Hike Strong
The Complete Guide to Building Mountain Strength, Endurance, and Confidence for Hiking and Backpacking

James Appleton

ESSEX, CONNECTICUT

FALCONGUIDES®

An imprint of The Globe Pequot Publishing Group, Inc.
64 South Main Street
Essex, CT 06426
www.globepequot.com

Falcon and FalconGuides are registered trademarks and Make Adventure Your Story is a trademark of The Globe Pequot Publishing Group, Inc.

Copyright © 2026 by James Appleton
Photos by Jonathan Zaharek unless otherwise noted

Cover photo by Mark Anderson

All rights reserved. No part of this book may be reproduced in any form or by any electronic or mechanical means, including information storage and retrieval systems, without written permission from the publisher, except by a reviewer who may quote passages in a review.

British Library Cataloguing-in-Publication Information available

Library of Congress Cataloging-in-Publication Data available

ISBN 978-1-4930-9211-6 (paper)
ISBN 978-1-4930-9212-3 (electronic)
ISBN 978-1-4930-9850-7 (hc)

Limit of Liability / Disclaimer of Warranty: The author and The Globe Pequot Publishing Group, Inc. (GPPG) expressly disclaim any and all liability for the use of any materials, information, or methods described in this book, including, without limitation, for accidents, injuries, illnesses, damages, or death sustained by readers who engage in the activities described or promoted herein. No representations or warranties are made as to the accuracy or completeness of the contents of this work, and all warranties, express or implied—including, without limitation, warranties of fitness for a particular purpose—are expressly disclaimed. The opinions presented are solely those of the author and are provided for informational purposes only.

Endorsement Disclaimer: Reference to any individual, organization, website, or other resource in this book does not constitute an endorsement by the author or GPPG of such party or the information, products, or services they may provide, now or in the future.

Disclaimer

The information provided in *Hike Strong* is intended for educational and informational purposes only and is not intended as medical advice, diagnosis, or treatment. The exercises, training protocols, and nutrition strategies discussed in this book are based on the author's personal experience and professional knowledge as a strength and conditioning coach, but they may not be suitable for everyone.

Always consult with your physician or a qualified healthcare provider before beginning any new exercise program, especially if you have any pre-existing medical conditions, injuries, or concerns about your physical health. The author and publisher are not responsible or liable for any injury, illness, or damages that may occur through the use or misuse of the information contained in this book.

All readers who engage in any activities or recommendations described herein do so at their own risk. Individual results may vary and are dependent on many factors including but not limited to adherence, effort, and baseline fitness.

Listen to your body, use good judgment, and prioritize safety in all physical activities.

Contents

Chapter 1. The Trailhead 1

Chapter 2. The Approach: Warm-Up 6

    Bonking, Trail Fails, and Heavy Breathing: James's Story 6

    How Strength Training Led Me to the Outdoors: James's
    Redemption 9

Chapter 3. The Ascent: Strength Training for Stronger Hiking 14

    The Biggest Myths in Hiking Preparation 14

    The Mountain-Strength Method: How to Train for the
    Demands of the Backcountry 19

    Building Strength 101 23

    Key Hiking Muscles 26

    Mountain-Strength Method Part 2: Elevation Days:
    Athleticism for the Backcountry 45

    Mountain-Strength Method Part 3: Approach Days:
    Endurance Training for Long Miles 50

    Mountain-Strength Method Part 4: Backpack Days: Building
    Backpack Strength for Hiking 53

    Common Mistakes Hikers Make When Strength Training 54

Chapter 4. The Refuel: Nutrition, Hydration, and Recovery 62

    Hiking on Empty in the Adirondack High Peaks 62

    Nutrition for Training and Life 64

    Hydration 78

    On-Trail Nutrition Strategy 85

    Recovery: The Most Overlooked Factor in Trail Readiness 93

Chapter 5. The Trail Split: Mindset for the Mountains 101

    The Mountains Are the Ultimate Equalizer .103

    Building Mental Toughness for the Backcountry—and Your Life 104

    Five Life Lessons from the Trail 110

Chapter 6. The Final Ascent: Six-Week Training Programs. 115

    Official Mountain-Strength Training Programs 118

    DIY Training Templates 169

Chapter 7. The Summit. 173

    Becoming Unstoppable—on the Trail and in Your Life 173

    Mountain-Strength Success Stories 176

The Descent 183

About the Author 184

Work with James. 186

Hike Strong Exercise Library 189

Acknowledgments 196

This book is dedicated to all of my **Great Range Athlete** and **Seek To Do More** clients around the United States and Canada who trusted me to help them build strength, endurance, and resilience for their adventures. May you all continue living a fulfilling life in the outdoors where your fitness and mindset never hold you back.
Keep moving forward and I'll see you on the trails!

Members of James's Great Range Athlete teams on group hikes together following their six-week online training programs.

Chapter 1

The Trailhead

In hiking, the *trailhead* is the starting point—the place where you sign in, throw on your backpack, and take your first steps into the unknown. It's where the adventure begins.

For the better part of my life I had more trail failures than trail successes. I bet you didn't expect this book to start with that sentence, but that's just the honest truth. I didn't grow up crushing summits or loving hiking despite growing up in the Adirondacks where climbing mountains is part of the culture. For years, hiking felt more like a punishment than an adventure. Anytime I got roped into a hike I was always the one falling behind, gasping for air, legs burning with every step, wondering why I even said yes in the first place.

And when I did agree to go hiking I wasn't out there hiking massive mountains either. I'm talking peaks most people would call "moderate"—popular day hikes that others seemed to breeze up while I was simply trying not to die. Every hike was always a struggle. I hated it. The bugs, the mud, the sweat, the steep climbs, the extra heavy breathing. My body was never ready for it, which is why every step always felt harder than it needed to be.

Because here's the thing no one ever wants to say out loud: **Hiking kind of sucks when you're not in shape for it.**

It's tough on the body.
It's done in uncomfortable conditions.
And to add insult to injury—no one is *making* you do it.

Hiking truly is a unique "sport" that requires a unique brand of physical fitness.

So when your body isn't ready for the physical demands of the trail, every step feels ten times harder. And that's exactly how I experienced hiking for years. That's why I hated it and avoided it altogether. I even abandoned my friends and turned around on one occasion an hour into a full-day hike because I couldn't handle it. More on that story later though.

But then two words changed everything: strength training.

Strength training opened the doors to the Great Outdoors in my life. And it can do the same for you.

Getting strong and fit flipped the switch not only for my hiking ability but for my whole life. Suddenly, my body could take me where I wanted to go. This "hiking thing" didn't feel like suffering anymore. It finally became something I actually enjoyed because I stopped surviving the trail and started thriving on it.

The transformation didn't happen overnight, but once it did, life looked different. I went from dragging myself up short trails to confidently summiting ten mountains in a single day. I could finally keep up, move well, carry my pack, and have fun hiking. I no longer had anxiety about my fitness at any trailhead. My body became my biggest asset instead of my biggest limitation. That's when the mountains became my life's playground.

And now, over a decade later—after summiting hundreds of mountains, guiding others into the backcountry, and coaching hundreds of hikers around the country to build strong, trail-ready bodies—I can tell you with full confidence that building the right kind of strength and conditioning for the trail is the cheat code for stronger hiking adventures.

That's why I wrote this book. Because I want you to experience the trail and the transformation that comes with it the same way I did.

Now here's another hard truth that most hikers aren't told:

The fancy gear in your backpack is irrelevant if your legs and lungs can't take you to the summit.

Let's unpack that—literally.

You can have the most popular backpack stuffed with the latest and greatest ultralight gear, but are your **back and core strong enough** to carry that pack pain free mile after mile?

You can have the trendy new trail runners or the best hiking boots money can buy, but are your **legs and lungs** strong and conditioned enough to even handle steep climbs, rugged terrain, and long descents?

Trekking poles are awesome tools, but is your **upper body strong enough** to maneuver your body across tough backcountry terrain—over boulders, under blowdown, up steep rock slabs—all with a fully loaded pack strapped to your back?

You can buy the most advanced water filter available, but do you know what your **body needs** to actually stay **hydrated** on the trail?

And yeah, lightweight, ultra-calorie-dense snacks are great—but does your **nutrition strategy** fuel you properly so you perform your best during the hike and recover well after?

You get the point. And don't get me wrong—gear is important. Very important. But it's secondary. **Your body is the most important piece of equipment on any hike.**

Grab a highlighter and highlight this next statement:

Fitness first. Gear second.

The outdoor industry and YouTube want you to believe gear is what gets you to the summit. And it's easy to fall into that trap because buying gear is convenient. It's fun. Gear requires zero effort. But it's your body that takes every step and carries you across every ridgeline. Unlike gear, you can't buy fitness. You have to earn it. It requires hard work, dedication, and consistency. But that's why you're here, right?

This book exists to help you do exactly that—to prepare the body wearing the backpack.

So first, let me say this: **Congratulations.**

The fact that you're reading this means you've already recognized that physical preparation matters. Well done on being ahead of the curve. You understand that in order to hike stronger, go farther, and enjoy your adventures more, you need to build a body capable of handling whatever the trail throws at you.

This isn't just a generic fitness book. This is a **trail-specific strength and conditioning plan** written by someone who lives and breathes both the gym and the mountains. As a hiking guide and strength coach, I've spent years combining these worlds for clients around the country—and now I'm sharing my blueprint with you.

Inside this book, you'll find a complete strategy from training, to nutrition, to mindset, and more. A step-by-step process to prepare your body for the rigors of long miles, steep climbs, and rugged backcountry terrain. Whether you're gearing up for a long-distance thru-hike on the AT or PCT, climbing the Adirondack High Peaks, the Whites, the Rockies, or simply looking for better weekend adventures on your local trails—this book will show you how to train *smarter* so you can hike *stronger*.

By the end of this book, you'll not only understand **what to train and how to train** but also **why it matters** and **how** it will transform your hiking ability.

Because the better we prepare, the better we perform. And the better we perform, the more fulfilling our outdoor adventures become.

No more trailhead anxiety wondering *"Am I fit enough for this hike?"*

Now you have the map to become the strong, confident, and capable hiker you deserve to be.

Stronger hiking adventures await you. Let's sign in and get started.

HIKE STRONG TRAIL REGISTER

NAME	ADDRESS	DATE	DESTINATION
			Strong Hiking Adventures
			Strong Hiking Adventures
			Strong Hiking Adventures

Yes, grab a pencil and literally sign in. This signature also serves as a commitment to yourself to do the work ensuring you're physically prepared *before* you head into the backcountry, so that your fitness becomes your biggest asset.

In this book you'll learn

- how to build functional, trail-specific strength
- how to develop endurance and stamina for long miles and steep climbs
- how to train your core and back to support a heavy backpack
- how to prepare your body to move like an athlete over rugged terrain
- how to fuel and hydrate your body for performance and recovery
- how to train your mind to push through hard climbs and tough conditions
- how to take the lessons from the backcountry and apply them to life beyond the trail

The author while guiding on the summit of Rocky Peak Ridge in the Adirondack High Peaks. Credit: Patrick Rohr.

CHAPTER 2

The Approach: Warm-Up

In hiking terms, the *approach* is the initial stretch of trail that leads from the trailhead to the base of the climb. It's the introduction or warm-up phase where your body gets moving and your mind locks in before the real ascent begins.

BONKING, TRAIL FAILS, AND HEAVY BREATHING: JAMES'S STORY
Have you ever been miles deep hiking in the backcountry and had your body stop working? Your brain is telling your legs to step, but your legs won't move? It's a scary and bizarre feeling. I do not recommend it. Before we get into that pivotal story though, let's backtrack and start from the beginning.

I grew up in the Adirondack Mountains of northern New York State in the heart of the 6.1-million-acre outdoor paradise known as the Adirondack Park in a town called Lake Placid. No, not the alligator movie, but yes the town where the 1980 "Miracle on Ice" took place during the 1980 Winter Olympics when Team USA hockey beat Russia.

For context, the Adirondack Park—a state park made up of public and private land—is the largest publicly protected wilderness in the contiguous United States and is larger than Yellowstone, Yosemite, Grand Canyon, Glacier, Everglades, and Great Smoky Mountains National Parks *combined*. Yes, it's that big and it's in New York State. In fact it's larger than five states. It's an outdoors mecca as wild as anything you'll ever experience and a place unlike any other in the United States.

As far as outdoor recreation is concerned, it's the primary place people from the northeast visit thanks to thousands of miles of trails, thousands of mountains, and thousands of lakes, rivers, and streams. Now that you have an understanding of the place where I grew up, you'll understand why hiking mountains is part of the culture here. This park and the towns within it revolve around the mountains. Lake Placid is the quintessential "sporty"

The Approach: Warm-Up

mountain town. You'll never drive anywhere without seeing someone running or bicycling or passing another car with a kayak or skis on the roof.

But as a punk rock kid, the beauty was lost on me because hiking up mountains was hard and I didn't care. In fact, the view of the Adirondack High Peaks outside the windows of my high school is so mind blowing it's hard to describe, yet the mountains were just a backdrop in my mind.

Now back to the story where my legs stopped working . . .

I was in my mid-twenties, sitting just around three hundred pounds of undisciplined laziness. Far removed from my days playing sports and riding BMX throughout high school. My brother and his wife invited me to go hike a medium-sized mountain here in the Adirondacks called McKenzie Mountain. Because this wasn't one of the forty-six High Peaks, I thought to myself, "Oh, it's not a High Peak, so it's probably easy. Sure!" I joined them for this 6.5-mile, 2,100-foot-elevation-gain hike. Cue the ominous music score where you know trouble is coming for the protagonist . . . dun-dun-dun . . .

We met at the trailhead and started hiking. My brother and his wife were properly prepared with all the right "stuff" in their backpacks. Me? I had a small water bottle and a granola bar. Yes, I was *that* guy. I didn't know any better at the time though, and I was thinking that because this mountain is "small," the hike would be "easy." Continue the ominous music score build . . .

The hike was, in fact, not easy. It was brutal for me, but I made it to the summit. It may have been ugly, but I was able to stumble my way to the top . . . barely. There I was on the summit of McKenzie, out of water, zero snacks in my pack, too embarrassed to ask my older brother to share some of his food and drink. I thought to myself, "Well, the hard work for the day is done, now the easy part going back down. I'll be fine." Famous last words. We began our descent.

After a couple miles of slow, technical hiking we made it down the mountain and all we had left were a couple miles of rolling trail back to the trailhead. My body was feeling the severe dehydration that was setting in thanks to my lack of fluids, salt, food, and my overall nonexistent physical fitness. Then it happened . . .

As the three of us walked down the trail, miles deep in the McKenzie Mountain Wilderness, my legs stopped working. "What is happening . . . this is weird," I thought to myself. My body turned off mid-step as sudden as the flip of a light switch. My legs literally would not move even though my brain was telling them to move. This can't be good . . .

I was in sight but well behind my brother and his wife as they continued hiking, completely unaware of what was unfolding behind them. Unable to move even one step, I yelled out to them, "Hey, guys, stop. Something's wrong . . ." They walked back to me and I explained what was going on. I didn't know if I was dying or what in the world was happening. Amy, being a physical therapist, knew exactly what was happening. I was severely dehydrated. I was "bonking."

So "bonking," a term used often in hiking, happens when your body runs out of energy entirely. The energy in your body and muscles is completely depleted, out of gas, and you hit a wall. Your car has hit empty and you're now broken down on the side of the highway. Bonking is more than just being fatigued; it's extreme fatigue and results in the sudden inability to do anything. Oh, and when I say sudden, I *mean* sudden. The whole day led me to this point, but the moment where I hit that wall was as sudden as literally the moment of impact hitting a wall.

Thanks to Joey and Amy being more experienced and prepared hikers than I was at the time, they knew exactly what I needed. I proceeded to drink every drop of liquid they had from Gatorade to water and devoured every calorie in both their packs in record time. About fifteen minutes later I was able to start moving again slowly and we finished the last couple miles out of the woods. It was slow going, but thankfully I avoided a much worse situation thanks to the preparation and guidance from my brother and sister-in-law. I will never forget that feeling where I was telling my legs to walk and they wouldn't move. Again, it's a bizarre and scary feeling and a moment that has stuck with me ever since.

At the end of the day my body was not prepared in any capacity for the hike, from my fitness to my nutrition, and I paid the price. It could have also been a lot worse for me, but thankfully the backcountry showed me a tad bit of grace that day. The mountains are no place to show up unprepared physically because they can literally kill you. I was fortunate that day but my problems were entirely my own fault and completely avoidable. This was only one of many trail fails I've had over the years thanks to my poor physical fitness and you'll read more of those stories throughout the book.

Now that you have an idea of where it all started, it's time for the redemption story.

How Strength Training Led Me to the Outdoors: James's Redemption

One fateful night in December 2014, a few years removed from bonking on McKenzie Mountain and just three months after my first daughter was born, my wife asked me a question that changed the trajectory of my life forever.

"James . . . I need to talk to you. . . . What's your endgame here? We have a daughter now . . ."

She was lovingly referring to the fact that I was a mess physically (three hundred pounds of laziness); I was a twenty-eight-year-old man-child, and the nine months leading up to our daughter's birth weren't the wakeup call for me she hoped they would be.

Ouch. That stung. But I deserved it. I needed it.

Trap bar deadlift. One of the most functional exercises and a staple in James's training programs.

Embarrassed and ashamed of myself, I rolled over, grabbed my flip phone off the nightstand, and texted a friend who was in great shape.

"Hey man, I need some help . . ."

Now cue the *Rocky* theme music.

It was time to go to work. So I did. And to this very day as you read this book, the work has never stopped. Thanks to consistency, determination, and grit, over the next few years I underwent the physical and mental transformation my life needed. I dropped nearly one hundred pounds, built strength and muscle, rewired my brain to do hard things, and finally became the man my growing family deserved.

Fast-forward a couple years, thanks to my newfound fitness level, I decided to revisit this "hiking thing" on a beautiful bluebird spring day in the Adirondacks. It had been years since I went hiking, and the last time I did go I turned around because it was "too hard." But I thought things would be different now. And they were.

The mountain was Ampersand Mountain. Another medium-sized peak for the area not far from my house. I arrived at the trailhead at 7:00 a.m. that sunny May morning. The birds were chirping, the trees were green, the sky was blue, and I was ready to start hiking. So I signed in, and off I went.

Less than two hours later after zero stops, zero heavy breathing, and zero other hikers, I stepped onto the open rock summit. The 2.7 miles and 1,800 feet of elevation were complete. I was shocked. I couldn't believe that I made it up with such ease without ever needing to stop. No hike had ever felt like that.

As I stood there on the summit eating leftover beef and rice in a Tupperware (not a fun hiking food choice but nutritional nonetheless), I looked out at the mountain views. A newfound awe had struck me. Suddenly hiking mountains *could* be fun and enjoyable instead of a miserable experience. The trail felt different that day. The mountains looked different. They felt obtainable now. All because I was finally in the right shape to enjoy the experience. On top of that, my brain could now handle doing hard things. I could power through challenges and keep going even when it got hard—something that plagued me before. Standing on that summit of Ampersand Mountain is a moment and feeling I'll remember forever.

I cruised down the mountain with ease and a newfound purpose. I passed other hikers on the descent, got back to the trailhead, and drove home with a smile on my face after a hike for the first time ever. I even deadlifted later that day too—because it was deadlift day and you don't skip deadlift day, right?

The following day I hiked Scarface Mountain, and the day after that I climbed St. Regis Mountain to become an official "Saranac Lake 6'er." I hiked three mountains in three days. Who was I? The doors of mountain adventure had finally been unlocked and they were wide open. The following week I officially began hiking the forty-six Adirondack High Peaks, a journey that changed the trajectory of my life.

After almost thirty years of living in the Adirondacks and hearing stories of people becoming an "Adirondack 46'er" (which is a person who summits all forty-six High Peaks in the Adirondacks) for the first time ever I was confident that I could do that too. I hiked the forty-six High Peaks from start to finish that summer, a transformative journey that changed how I view the mountains, hiking, the outdoors, and life in general and a journey that molded me into the man I am today.

The Approach: Warm-Up

Lunges. One of the best exercises to build trail-ready legs.

The doors to the great outdoors opened when I made the choice to change and put in the hard work to get strong and fit for my life. A new world of adventure was suddenly at my fingertips, and over a decade later I've never looked back. Now I even have the privilege of helping others feel that same confidence so they can experience that same transformation too. I thank the good Lord above for blessing me with the path that led me to the mountains. It was a windy, muddy, rugged path, but aren't they all? Life in the backcountry and life in the real world aren't all that different when you think about it.

HOT TAKE: The Mountains Are NOT Calling You . . .

I want you to picture walking down your favorite trail for a moment. Notice the smells of the spruce and pine trees as a light breeze blows across on your face. The evergreens sway as the leaves blow off the hardwoods and the golden sun shines down through the canopy. Imagine glancing off the trail to your left and notice how the trees align in the woods. Now imagine again taking five more steps forward and glancing to your left again. Suddenly those exact same woods look different because the trees align differently. They're the same woods, same trees, but viewed from a fresh perspective.

With this in mind I'd like to invite you to take on a new perspective about the mountains and the famous yet often misused 1873 quote from the legendary John Muir:

"The mountains are calling and I must go . . ."

Hot Take:
The mountains don't care about you.

This quote is often taken out of context in the hiking world. The mountains are *not* calling you. They will chew you up and spit you out if you're not properly prepared for them. They'll remain unchanged whether you ever go hiking or not . . . and that's a great thing.

Fresh Take:
The mountains allow you the *privilege* to explore them.

They're in charge—not you.

Going into the backcountry is not something to be taken lightly or for granted. Having the physical ability to experience those views in person—views that most will only see through pictures—is something to be grateful for. It's a privilege, plain and simple. When we shift our perspective from feeling like the *"mountains are calling us"* to *"it's a privilege to explore them,"* our demeanor shifts. The way we view them and prepare for them shifts. We become more willing to go the extra mile to ensure we're living up to that privilege. We no longer view the mountains from a sense of entitlement, as if they exist for our benefit, but rather from a place of reverence and admiration. It's kind of like when someone invites you to join their family for Thanksgiving dinner. You don't show up looking like someone who's been on the trail for two weeks straight, empty handed, unshowered, and unkempt (well, I hope you don't anyways). Instead you show up, side dish in hand, cleaned up, on your best behavior, and grateful to be there because it's a privilege to be invited.

I encourage you to adopt this perspective shift because it's going to lay a strong foundation for how you approach your fitness and physical preparedness for hiking and backpacking. Think of the mountains as the coach who inspires you to play harder, or the amazing boss who leads by example that you're willing to go above and beyond for.

The Approach: Warm-Up

You're preparing for the privilege of exploring the beauty of the backcountry, and you ought to be your best out there. In the end you owe it to yourself and the trail to show up at your best. Because the mountains are certainly going to give you their best every time.

Next Steps

1. Assess your current fitness level (not where it used to be, where it is *today*).
2. Commit to yourself to not only read the book through but also to immediately execute the plan within it.
3. Hold yourself accountable to do the hard work in the gym and in the kitchen, even on the days you don't feel like it.

Time to Get Strong

Now that you know what to expect in this book and who I am, it's time to get to work. Think of this book as your training partner, trail map, and guide rolled into one. In the next chapter I'll introduce you to the Mountain-Strength Method so you can start building strength, endurance, and resilience for longer, stronger hikes.

Because *stronger* adventures are *better* adventures. Let's begin the climb.

James standing on the summit of Mt. Colvin on a bluebird summer day.

CHAPTER 3

The Ascent: Strength Training for Stronger Hiking

IN HIKING, THE *ASCENT* REFERS TO THE PART OF THE TRAIL THAT GOES UP the mountain and where the real climbing begins. The terrain gets steeper, the heavy breathing increases, and the hard work sets in, requiring strength, endurance, and determination to get you to the summit.

> *Strength training is the foundation of good fitness because it improves so many things at once. It builds both upper and lower body strength, boosts endurance, and improves stability which are all qualities hikers need out on the trail. It also lowers your risk of injury because it makes your muscles, joints, tendons, and ligaments more resilient. Furthermore, it helps you fight off fatigue so you can ultimately stay out in the mountains longer—and that's what it's all about.*
> —Kieran Brennan, MS, NSCA CSCS, USAW L-2, USATF L-1, FRCms Director of Performance, Combine Training (Greenwich, Connecticut)

Kieran is an avid hiker, powerlifter, and professional strength and conditioning coach who works with Olympians and professional, collegiate, and high school athletes and was a former assistant strength and conditioning coach for Team USA Bobsled & Skeleton (USABS).

THE BIGGEST MYTHS IN HIKING PREPARATION
MYTH 1: Gear matters more than fitness.

There's a statistic that goes around the internet stating that roughly 20 percent of Appalachian Trail thru-hikers quit at Neel Gap, a mere 31 miles into the almost 2,200-mile trail. Of course, there are many reasons why people quit, but I'm willing to bet that if more of those hikers had properly prepared their bodies ahead of time by getting stronger, more conditioned, and ready for the unique physical toll of backpacking, those numbers would be a lot lower. I'm also willing to bet most of them have the latest, greatest gear in their backpacks. Too bad the gear in your pack doesn't matter if your body can't carry you through the trail, right?

Your physical ability will be the biggest determining factor to your success in the backcountry. A strong, conditioned, resilient body is your best asset. Like we discussed earlier, fitness first, gear second.

MYTH 2: More cardio is the best way to prepare for hiking.

Let's talk about cardio. Most people assume the best way to get ready for a hike is to start running more, biking more, or adding in hours upon hours of steady-state cardio. They think because they always struggle up steep climbs it means they need to do more cardio. If this sounds familiar, I'd like to set you free because you have been lied to. You're not training to run a marathon; you're preparing to traverse the rugged terrain of the backcountry. In fact, if your training plan does look like a marathoner's prep schedule, I hate to break it to you, but you're actually sabotaging your own hiking performance.

That nonstop cardio is actually burning away the very muscle you need to power up those steep climbs and carry that heavy backpack. Cardio doesn't make your body stronger; it makes your heart stronger. And don't get me wrong: Having a strong heart and a good aerobic base is obviously important, and we'll train for that too—but there's more to the hiking equation than just a strong heart. A lot more. Strength is what keeps your body resilient *while* you're logging those miles. Plus, strength training will get your heart *and* your body stronger at the same time. That's a lot more efficient, wouldn't you agree?

In the end, we need muscle mass to perform optimally. Nonstop cardio doesn't prevent burning quads on the ascent or sore knees on the descent. It won't stabilize your hips, knees, and ankles when you're crossing rivers, climbing boulders, or jumping down ledges. And it certainly won't help you carry that thirty-pound pack up a steep ridge. Strength is what allows your body to do the work—cardio is just what keeps you going. That's why so many hikers feel like they're doing "all the right things" in their training but still feel underpowered once they hit real elevation gain. They're usually missing the strength piece.

MYTH 3: The only way to get in shape for hiking is by going hiking.

Yes and no. If you live in an outdoors paradise like I do where there are thousands of miles of trails, hundreds of mountains big and small, and dozens of trailheads within a fifty-mile radius of all difficulty levels, that could be an option. Hiking smaller mountains and gradually hiking bigger ones over time is certainly a valid approach. Most people, however, don't live in an area where it's even an option, and that's why strategically training beforehand will only benefit you on the trail. This way you'll skip the early stages of hiking misery so many of us have endured by not being physically ready for this endeavor.

Many backpackers like to think they'll "find their trail legs" on the trail and therefore they do little to no preparation before their long-distance trek. What a poor strategy. The more work you do ahead of time to set yourself up for success, the higher your odds of success.

Time on your feet on the trail is important, and the most optimal approach would be to do both—hike and train. If hiking isn't possible, however, strategic strength training is the answer. Elite athletes strength train for their sports, so we should too.

Speaking of athletes . . .

MYTH 4: Hiking is not an athletic endeavor.

Hiking is a full-body strength and conditioning event cleverly disguised as a recreational activity. Especially if you're hiking up mountains. Funny how that happens, right? After all, you're not just taking a stroll on a gentle trail at your local dog park—you're climbing elevation, crossing flowing rivers, lunging, jumping, bracing, and balancing, all while carrying a loaded backpack over uneven terrain where one misstep can become a major problem. It requires strong legs, back, and shoulders; a stable core; durable joints; and a level of muscular endurance reminiscent of any athletic pursuit. On top of that you're doing it in an environment that can literally kill you. All the more reason to have the ability to move like an athlete.

Athletes train for everything from strength, to endurance, to agility so they perform at their best on the field or court. They're ready for anything. When hikers train the same way they become better prepared for whatever the trail throws at them.

THE ANSWER: Train like a strong, well-rounded mountain athlete.

It's time to start thinking and training like a "mountain athlete." Hiking may not have a ball—though I wish there was a "hiking ball"—but it is undoubtedly a sport and should be treated as an athletic pursuit. Everything should be trained accordingly from pure strength, to conditioning, to "strength-and-conditioning," to long-distance endurance, and more to meet the demands you'll encounter on the "field" (aka the trail).

So if you are a cardio rat it's time to replace many of those long, boring cardio sessions with strength-focused work that builds your muscles, strengthens your joints, and progresses weekly—things like weighted step-ups, heavy rucks, squats, lunges, deadlifts, presses, and bodyweight training are great ways to do that. Your primary goal should be to get strong, conditioned, and athletic for the unique demands of the trail.

Hiking has very few redeeming qualities if every step feels like death—I've been there. But when your body is strong, conditioned, athletic, and resilient, it becomes an adventure that always has you coming back for more. Getting strong will unlock a version of hiking you didn't even know was possible.

Mountain Shape Versus Regular Shape

Over the years I've had several marathon runners reach out to me letting me know two things:

1. How many marathons they've run.
2. Despite running said marathons, hiking the Adirondack Mountains (where I'm based) kicked their butt beyond what they ever expected.

Now most people would agree that a marathon runner is well above average when it comes to fitness. So how did the mountains humble these above-average athletes so much? It's simply because the mountains require a unique brand of physical fitness.

Being "in shape" and being in "mountain shape" are different. One isn't better than the other; they're just different. Of course, if your goals and joys are found hiking, then one might be better than the other for you, but the point is that they're different. And different sports have different needs.

I've also found that people who are slightly out of shape but have backcountry experience tend to perform better than people in great shape who've never hiked before. I believe it has to do with the mental aspect of knowing what to expect. They know how the trail impacts their body, what steep ascents/descents and long miles feel like, and how to pace themselves out there. These are big factors for success. The mental part of the game is huge, but we'll get to that later in the book.

Squats. The king of exercises.

Whether you're hiking mountains, running a marathon, mountain biking, playing basketball, powerlifting, or whatever else your physical endeavors look like, I believe you should build a solid foundation of pure, functional strength first and foremost.

A strong body leads to strong adventures, and strong adventures are exactly what we're here to have.

HIKING = "TYPE 2" FUN

Sometimes hiking is very fun in the moment, but at the end of the day I'd classify the sport of hiking on the whole as "Type 2" fun. Type 2 fun means it's not always enjoyable during the experience but becomes more enjoyable and rewarding afterward due to the sense of accomplishment and the stories it provides. Hard now, but fun to talk about later. Think about it, you're choosing to traverse miles through the woods wearing a loaded backpack, sweating and breathing heavily with burning muscles. And you're going to do this in dirty, wet, muddy, bug-infested conditions, while the hot sun beats down on you in the summer or the cold wind whips across your face in the winter. The terrain is steep, rugged, uneven, and often unforgiving. Then you're going to sleep on the ground or on a wooden shelter floor for days, weeks, or, for the hardcore folks, even months at a time while eating food you wouldn't even consider under "normal" circumstances. All in the name of "fun" and "adventure." That's classic Type 2 fun if you ask me. We're all a little bit crazy when you stop and think about it. Hiking is wild—no pun intended (just kidding, please intend the pun).

At the end of the day, climbing mountains or backpacking long trails is a task no one is making you do. You're choosing to do it. So if your body and mind aren't ready for the ups and downs of the journey, it might not be that joyful and romantic experience the books and social media pages make it out to be. It could be—but it also might be a brutal grind that turns you off from hiking and the outdoors altogether. And we definitely don't want that.

It's time to start building the strength and endurance that improve your ability on the trail so your adventures become everything you hoped for. First, let's talk about the different types of physical demands you should train for and how we're going to train for each. **Welcome to the Mountain-Strength Method.**

The author while backpacking the 138-mile Northville-Placid Trail. Credit: Josh Bliss.

THE MOUNTAIN-STRENGTH METHOD: HOW TO TRAIN FOR THE DEMANDS OF THE BACKCOUNTRY

As I said earlier, hiking is a unique "sport" with its own unique challenges. So when your training accounts for those challenges, your performance will dramatically improve. It's an amazing feeling when you start hiking up a steep section of trail that you expect yourself to struggle on but instead your heart, legs, and lungs power up with no issue. The first time you experience this it will likely leave you both confused and excited at how "easy" it was. It's a great feeling.

The **Mountain-Strength Method** includes four pillars and ensures no stone is left unturned in your trail fitness. If you focus on improving all four of these categories you'll become unstoppable on any trail. To accomplish this, each of these pillars gets its own dedicated training day. If you skip over any of these pillars, however, the trail will let you know of your blunder. So that's why we're going to make sure everything gets strong at once.

The four pillars of the **Mountain-Strength Method** are

1. Foundational Strength
2. Elevation Athleticism
3. Trail Endurance
4. Backpack Strength

Next let's break down these four pillars, why you're training this way, and how they'll impact your ability in the backcountry.

1. FOUNDATIONAL STRENGTH, aka "Mountain-Strength Days"

What: "Mountain-Strength" days are where we build your **foundational strength**. This is the same for life as it is for the mountains. It's the foundation of your training that everything else builds off. Building a stronger body should be the goal of your training: stronger muscles, joints, tendons, ligaments, heart, lungs, and mind.

Why: Being strong top to bottom makes us safer and more physically competent in the backcountry. We should aim to be classified as *"strong"* period, not just *"strong . . . for a hiker."* Whether you're training for backpacking or football, the foundational principles of building strength will remain, and the stronger your entire body is the better you'll perform. Plus, a strong body has a much lower likelihood of "breaking" in backcountry.

How: We'll accomplish this by implementing a strength training protocol that makes sure no muscle groups are left behind. Yes, that includes strengthening your upper body too. However, you're going to strengthen these muscles in ways that also mimic the cardiovascular demands of the trail. Win-win.

Bottom Line: Hiking may seem like a "lower-body-only" sport, but it's not. It's a full-body pursuit. So you're not only getting your legs and lungs strong, you're getting your entire body strong top to bottom. A strong, wide foundation will let us build a big house on top of it.

2. ELEVATION ATHLETICISM, aka "Elevation Days"

What: Elevation days improve your "strength and conditioning," or, as I prefer to call it, your **athleticism**. Yes, athleticism. Some people are surprised when I say hiking demands the ability to move like an athlete, but it's the truth. After all, you're navigating your body up and over uneven backcountry terrain, breathing heavily with burning muscles, all while wearing a loaded backpack. I'd say that makes it quite the athletic endeavor.

Elevation days are a true hybrid strength and conditioning builder because you're improving both your muscular strength and muscular endurance simultaneously. Oh, you'll also be breathing heavily too. These sessions will have your anaerobic conditioning firing on all cylinders, which will serve you well during those steep climbs.

Why: From steep ascents and descents, to pulling yourself up by roots along the side of rock slabs, to maneuvering your body up and over boulders and blowdowns, having the strength, conditioning, and agility to effectively control your body is important for your success.

How: We'll accomplish this with bodyweight circuit training, also known as calisthenics, and dumbbell circuits. There's no better way to build the athleticism needed for hiking than by making you control your body in an athletic manner while also improving your strength and conditioning at the same time.

Bottom Line: Backcountry travel is not the same as hiking a trail at the local dog park. Possessing a higher level of athleticism will always be an advantage on the trail.

3. TRAIL ENDURANCE, aka "Approach Days"

What: Approach days are where we improve your long-distance **endurance**. These training days seek to strengthen your heart health via steady-state cardio. While strength is your foundation, you still need to include plenty of aerobic training to build that trail endurance so you can handle long miles.

Why: Putting long miles on your feet in the woods is the name of the game here. Whether you're hiking eight miles just to the base of the mountain before ascending, climbing a steep slab, or logging twenty miles of rolling hills on your way to the next shelter, having the cardiovascular capacity to endure long days with an elevated heart rate is crucial. It's yet again another unique element of hiking that must be trained for.

How: We'll accomplish this through general steady-state cardio where the goal is to find a pace that challenges you, but is maintainable for a long distance, and then let it rip. I'm a big believer that the best "hiking pace" is going as fast as you *can* go but as slow as you *need* to go so that you never have to stop. That is the sweet spot in my experience.

Bottom Line: Hiking requires the ability to log long miles with an elevated heart rate. So we'll make sure your heart is just as strong as your legs. After all, your heart is a muscle too.

4. BACKPACK STRENGTH, aka "Backpack/Ruck Days"

What: These days are devoted to one purpose: time spent on your feet carrying a loaded backpack. The goal is to build "**backpack strength**" in your upper back, traps, shoulders, core, hips, legs, lungs, and heart so your pack weight is never a limiting factor. It's a very simple but important element to account for in the world of hiking strength.

Why: In everyday life, how often are you wearing a loaded backpack for hours, miles, or days at a time? Probably not too often. Building up your strength and tolerance for carrying a backpack mile after mile will serve you well on the trail. So you're going to account for this unique demand in your training too.

How: You'll accomplish this by including a structured ruck or hiking day each week wearing a heavy backpack. This can be completed on a trail or just walking around your neighborhood. Each week you'll log miles and aim to increase your speed, distance, and backpack weight. You'll want your ruck day pack to be heavier than your typical hiking pack, that way your backpack will feel light when you put it on at the trailhead.

Bottom Line: Your backpack is the mother ship on the trail, so it deserves dedicated training to ensure you can carry that weight. When you arrive on the trail you'll be glad your fully loaded backpack feels "light."

Now that you have a general understanding of the **Mountain-Strength Method** and what areas to focus on in your training, let's learn how to build strength so your training produces the results you're working hard for.

Building Strength 101

There's a big difference between "working out" and "training." People who "work out" are moving their body, burning some calories, and sweating, but they're not necessarily building anything. On the other hand, people who are "training" are strategically and methodically building their strength and ability. Moving forward I want you focused on "training" with intention, not aimlessly "working out." You can do that by following a plan that builds your strength strategically week after week.

I've coached hundreds of men and women over the years from first-time hikers to exceptionally experienced backpackers looking to improve their fitness for the trail. I've found people are always more successful when they have the basic understanding of the "why" behind the process. I won't dive too deep here, rather I'll keep it simple and give you the 101 version, but it's important information to learn.

When it all boils down, building strength can be summed up in two words: progressive overload. I know, big scary words, but don't let them frighten you. I'll explain . . .

Progressive Overload Simplified

"Progressive overload" is a very literal principle. You are "progressively" (aka little by little) increasing the total "load" (aka weight or reps) lifted over a period of time under the same conditions. That's it. You're gradually increasing the demands on your muscles and forcing them to adapt and grow. You'll accomplish this by adding weight, reps, or total number of sets on the same exercise each week.

Slow and steady wins the race here. Ultimately you're looking to see an increase in your ability compared to your last workout.

Here are some simplified examples of progressive overload so you can visualize it:

> Progressive Overload with **Weight:**
> Week 1 you lifted **100 pounds** for 5 reps. Week 2 you lifted **105 pounds** for 5 reps.
> Goal: Same number of sets and reps but with more weight

Progressive Overload with **Reps:**
Week 1 you lifted 100 pounds for **5 reps.** Week 2 you lifted 100 pounds for **6 reps**.
Goal: Same amount of weight and sets but with more reps

Progressive (Volume) Overload with **Total Sets:**
Week 1 you lifted 100 pounds for **3 sets** of 5 reps. Week 2 you lifted 100 pounds for **4 sets** of 5 reps.
Goal: Same amount of weight and reps but with more total sets

That wasn't so bad, right? These are the simple parameters of how to get stronger and fitter and build muscle for whatever your fitness goals involve. The goal is to consistently push yourself just beyond your current threshold week after week to generate growth.

Stronger Muscles = Longer Miles

In the end you must "progressively overload" your weights if you want your muscles to grow and get stronger. If you don't, your muscles have no incentive to grow. If you always lift the same weight, sets, and reps, your body is "working," but it's not necessarily growing because it doesn't need to. It isn't being forced to grow. Remember when I talked about the difference between "working out" and "training"? If you're not strategically overloading, you're only "working out," not "training."

By employing progressive overload principles week after week you're telling your muscles,

> *"Hey, this is harder than last week, but I still need you to lift this weight. Therefore you're going to have to grow bigger and stronger."*

Remember, there's never a downside to being strong because being strong makes the hard things easier. The stronger you are, the farther you can go in the mountains. That's what we're here to do. Stronger muscles give you the ability to enjoy longer mile hikes.

Now you might be wondering *"but how much weight should I lift?"* I'm glad you asked.

"How Much Weight Should I Lift?"

Building strength is like making s'mores around the campfire. If you try roasting the marshmallow holding it two feet from the flame, it will never cook. On the flip side, if you put it in the flame, it catches on fire, resulting in a disgusting black glob of burn. As any professional s'mores roaster knows, you want to hold the marshmallow *near* the flame but not in the flame, so it absorbs the heat of the fire without burning. The results? A delicious browned piece of campfire perfection. Training is the same way. You don't want to go so light that it doesn't help you, but you also don't want to go so heavy that it breaks you. Lift weights that challenge you for the prescribed rep range to generate growth. Think "moderate/heavy weight," not "light weight" and not "maximal weight."

With all of my clients I like to use a system called "Reps in Reserve" (RIR) because I've found it's the simplest approach. Reps in Reserve simply means how many more reps you could have lifted before muscular failure: the number of reps you still had "in reserve." For example, if you lift ten reps but you probably could have done two more reps, that would be "2 Reps in Reserve" or "2 RIR." It's an estimation, but over time you'll get good at judging that.

With all factors considered, in my experience the sweet spot is in the one to two RIR range. Choose weights that leave you in that ballpark and try to progressively overload them week after week for best results. Just think about making s'mores and getting that beautiful golden brown crust as you hold the marshmallow in the heat just outside the flame but not in it. Anyone else hungry now?

In the end your weights need to be aligned with the prescribed number of reps. **The lower the reps, the heavier the weight.** For example, if you're supposed to do a set of eight reps but you use a weight you could have done for fifteen reps, it's not heavy enough to give you the stimulus you're looking for. On the other hand, going too heavy or to total failure too often could potentially fry your central nervous system, resulting in a low quality performance later, and sometimes more injury risk.

Every rep range has its place, but because people like exact numbers, here are some good rep ranges to aim for.

The Mountain-Strength Sweet Spot:
Strength and Muscle: 5 to 8 reps per set in the 1 to 2 RIR range

Muscular Endurance: 10 to 15 reps per set in the 0 to 1 RIR range

You don't have to fear lifting heavy or going to muscular failure though. In fact you *must* lift heavy and close to failure in order to generate growth. Lifting heavy weights is also how you get the toned, muscular physique most people want. The idea of light weight for lots of reps to "tone" is another lie you've been told. Endless reps with light weights just adds excessive wear and tear on your joints with little to no muscular or strength benefits. Don't be afraid to lift heavy now so you can hike hard later.

Now that you understand the process and basic principle of building strength, let's move on to the key muscle groups that will propel you to the summit so you can get them all strong.

KEY HIKING MUSCLES

The "Average Joe" might be thinking your legs are the only muscles that matter when it comes to hiking, but "Average Joe" is wrong. In this section I'll go over the different muscle groups and where they come into play when hiking. There's a lot of muscles working together to move you from the trailhead to the summit. We'll start with your wheels, aka your legs, and work our way up.

Calves

What Calves Do: Your calf muscle supports you when you're standing and enables you to move your foot, ankle, and lower leg.

Why Calves Are Important on the Trail: It's your calves that push you forward when you walk. Pretty important for hiking, right? Calves allow you to jump, rotate your ankle, flex your foot, and lock your knee in place when you're enjoying those summit views too.

Exercises to Strengthen Calves

- Calf raises: standing holding weights or seated with weights on your legs
- Single-leg calf raises: perform on a stair for best stretch
- Farmer's carries: walking on your toes will emphasize the calf muscle more
- Jump squats

Goblet squats. A mountain-strength builder.

- Jump rope
- Jump lunges
- High knees

Quadriceps

What Quadriceps Do: The main function of your "quads" is to extend your leg at the knee, stabilize the knee, and flex your thigh at the hip. It's the big beefy muscle on the front of your thigh that runs from your hip to your knee.

Why Quads Are Important on the Trail: Every time you step up onto a rock on a trail, your quads are doing most of the work to stand back up. The quads are at play any time you're running, walking, or jumping. Talk about a prime hiking muscle. Strong quads help create strong knees too.

Exercises to Strengthen Quads

- Squats: all variations
- Leg extensions
- Step-ups

- Lunges: all variations
- Leg press: feet low for quad focus
- Squats (once again for good measure)

Hamstrings

What Hamstrings Do: Your hamstrings, aka "hammies," are a three-muscle group on the back of your thigh running down from the hip to just below your knee. Their role is to bend the knee and straighten your leg back at the hip.

Why Hamstrings Are Important on the Trail: Your hamstrings are what enable things like climbing, running, and jumping by essentially helping you bend your knee and straighten your leg at the hip. Imagine trying to hike a trail if you couldn't bend your knee or straighten your leg at the hip. Sounds like a rough time.

Exercises to Strengthen Hamstrings
- Deadlifts: barbell, trap bar, dumbbells
- Romanian deadlifts (RDL)
- Stiff-leg deadlifts
- Leg curls
- Glute-ham raise
- Kettlebell swings
- Good mornings
- Split squats
- Sumo squats
- Squats
- Glute bridges

Glutes

What Glutes Do: Your gluteal muscles' (aka your butt) primary function is to keep us upright and pushing our bodies forward. They stabilize the hips and support your lower back and spine, which therefore supports balance and general posture. Hard to climb a mountain with poor balance, right?

Why Glutes Are Important on the Trail: Glutes are the largest muscles in your body and some of the most important for a strong, healthy existence, on and off the trail. By keeping us upright and helping with forward movement, strong glutes are going to dramatically increase your hiking ability. On top of being the "power muscle," your glutes also serve as a shock absorber when you walk, run, or jump. Good muscle to have strong for those long miles in the woods.

Exercises to Strengthen Glutes

- Squats: all variations
- Deadlifts: all variations
- Lunges: all variations
- Hip thrust
- Glute bridges
- Good mornings
- Glute kickbacks
- Step-ups
- Kettlebell swings
- Clamshells
- Lateral band walks

Adductors and Abductors

What They Do: Your abductor and adductor muscles are located in your hips and thighs and work together to move your legs sideways. Your abductors are on the outside of your hips above your butt and are responsible for moving your leg away from your body. Your adductors are on your inner thigh and move the leg back in toward your body. Abductors move your leg out, adductors move it back in. Together these muscles play a crucial role in stabilizing your pelvis while walking, running, and jumping. You probably already know where I'm going with this one . . .

Why Abductors and Adductors Are Important on the Trail: Any muscles that help stabilize your pelvis for walking are vital given your hiking goals. Long miles expose weaker areas quickly and usually cause problems elsewhere. If your adductors and/or abductors are weak, your hips might not work properly and will force another part of your body to make up for the deficiency. For example, if your hips collapse it's going to force your knees, lower back, and lower limbs to work overtime, a recipe for an overuse injury given the miles we hikers put in. Strong muscles support strong joints, ultimately helping us avoid injury or pain. Hiking fifteen or twenty miles on the trail is hard enough, let alone having to deal with pain during those miles.

Exercises to Strengthen Abductor and Adductor

- Squats: wide stance
- Cossack squat
- Deadlifts: sumo stance
- Lateral band walks
- Side lunges
- Clamshells
- Adductor machine
- Side planks
- Standing/seated hip abduction with bands

Core: Abs, Obliques, Lower Back

What It Does: Your "core" is a general term referring to multiple muscles in your mid-section that work together, but its main duty is to stabilize your body by supporting your spine. For our purposes we'll just call this the "core" section. Your core transfers force between your upper and lower body so you move properly and helps prevent excessive strain on your back/spine. In simple terms, your core stabilizes your body. A strong core ensures your muscles do the stabilizing work, not your spine.

Why Your Core Is Important on the Trail: Your core connects your back holding your pack and your legs doing the hiking. Again, it's important to ensure these muscles are strong so that your spine isn't doing all the "heavy lifting." A "bad back" will lower your chances of success, so keeping your core muscles strong and healthy will make for a more enjoyable hiking experience and general existence.

Exercises to Strengthen Core

- Squats: back squats, front squats, or goblet squats
- Deadlifts: all variation
- Planks: all variations
- Weighted carries: all variations
- Farmer's walk
- Deadbugs
- Russian twists
- Bird dogs
- Push-ups
- Leg raises
- Cable crunches
- Reverse leg crunches
- Flutter kicks

Back: Upper, Mid, Low

What It Does: Having a strong back is a necessity for life. For our purposes we'll talk about your entire back as a whole. It's made up of many muscles (lats, traps, erectors, rhomboids, and levator scapulae). Ultimately your back muscles support your spine, attach your pelvis and shoulders to your torso, and provide mobility and stability to your torso and spine . . . oh, and it holds your backpack too, right?

Why Your Back Is Important on the Trail: Your back supports your spine, helps you stand upright and stable, and holds your backpack. As I mentioned, having a strong back is important for life, but when it comes to the trail it's even more important because we're wearing a heavy backpack mile after mile, day after day. Rarely in life do we ever wear a heavy backpack for hours or days on end, so intentionally strengthening these muscles is important. Your back also comes into play every time you use your trekking poles to help propel you up a ledge, over a stream, or any time you're using them to move forward. Having a strong back can be the deciding factor between a fulfilling day in the woods and a miserable one.

Exercises to Strengthen Your Back

- Rows: all variations
- Lat pull-downs: all variations
- Pull-ups: all variations
- Farmer's walk
- Weighted carries: all variations
- Deadlifts
- Squats
- Shrugs
- Band pull-aparts
- Planks

Shoulders

What They Do: Your shoulders move your arms. Like your "core" and "back," you're probably well aware there is no muscle called your "shoulder" muscle either. Rather the "shoulder joint" is made up of several muscles that work together to provide stability and movement within that area of your body. Some of these muscles include deltoids, rhomboids, rotator cuff muscles, trapezius, and many more. Entire books exist simply on this one area of the body, so it's quite complex. For our purposes again we'll generalize this area of your body.

Why Shoulders Are Important on the Trail: At first glance you may think your shoulders don't matter a whole lot for hiking, but I disagree. Having a foundation of strength top to bottom is going to make any adventure better. Having a "bad shoulder" can be devastating for everyday life activities, let alone out on the trail, ultimately keeping people in their living room instead of the backcountry. So strengthening this sensitive yet important part of the body will improve the quality of your performance and enjoyment. Strong shoulders are healthy shoulders, and I'd go as far as to say healthy shoulders are actually necessary for hiking. Anytime you have to maneuver your body over, under, up, or around boulders, blowdown, slabs, or ledges, your shoulders come into play. Your backpack straps also sit on your trapezius muscle (aka your "traps"), so pain in any of this area will hinder your experience. Anyone who's experienced shoulder pain knows how difficult simple mundane tasks become, let alone running around the mountains. So let's keep them strong and healthy.

Exercises to Strengthen Shoulders

- Overhead/military press: all variations
- Push-ups
- Lateral raises
- Rear delt flyes
- Front raises
- Face pulls
- Band pull-aparts
- Shrugs
- Dumbbell upright rows
- Band external rotations

Pectorals

What They Do: Your pectoral muscles, also known as "pecs," are a group of muscles in your chest that help with a variety of upper body movements from pushing and lifting to stabilizing and rotating your shoulders and arms. You may not think these muscles come into play during hiking, but you're probably realizing hiking is actually a full body sport. When everything is strong and supported, performance always improves.

Why Pecs Are Important on the Trail: On top of general support of your arms and shoulder, your chest comes into play every time you're using your trekking poles while descending. It's your chest that fires as you lean into your trekking poles and takes unnecessary pressure off your hips and knees while descending. A strong upper body will aid everything from holding your pack to maneuvering yourself up a ledge or slab.

Exercises to Strengthen Chest

- Bench press: barbell, dumbbell, incline, decline, flat; all variations, angles, and grips
- Chest flyes: all variations and angles

- Push-ups
- Dips

Arms

What They Do: Your "arms" are made up of many muscles from your biceps, to triceps, to forearms. These muscle groups all break down even further, but for our purposes we'll generalize them again. Your biceps' role is to bend your elbow and rotate your palm up. Triceps do the opposite, however; they straighten your elbow. Next, your forearm's job is to move your wrist, hand, and fingers all around, enabling things like gripping and turning your hand up or down.

Why Arms Are Important on the Trail: Your arms come into play every time you pick up your backpack or grab onto a root or tree to pull yourself up or lower yourself down a section. Trekking poles live in your hands and are maneuvered via your arms. Overall arm strength is certainly a worthwhile use of our training time, even for hiking. Remember your biceps bend your elbow, your triceps straighten your elbow, and your forearms help you grip and move your hand. Plus, no one's ever said, "I wish I *didn't* have strong, muscular arms," right?

Exercises to Strengthen Arms

- Biceps curls: all variations
- Triceps extensions
- Triceps push-downs
- Push-ups
- Pull-ups
- Dips
- Bench press
- Pull-downs
- Rows
- Farmer's walk: for grip strength
- Wrist curls
- Wrist extensions
- Bar hangs

Heart

What It Does: The heart is one muscle we certainly can't forget about. Technically it's considered a "muscular organ," but we all know it's the single most important muscle in our body. Its main role is to pump blood and oxygen around your body and to bring waste (aka carbon dioxide) back to the lungs to be removed from your body. If you wonder where the "heavy breathing" comes from while hiking or training, it's because your body needs more oxygen to fuel your working muscles; therefore, your heart has to work harder and pump blood faster. The "heavy breathing" is the result of your body needing to take in more oxygen to account for this. In short, it's your body's way of meeting the increased energy demands of physical activity. So the next time you're breathing heavily while climbing a steep section on a trail (or walking up those stairs at work), you'll know why.

Why Your Heart Is Important on the Trail: The stronger and more efficient your heart is, the further you'll be able to hike. When your heart is strong and in "good shape," you'll recover faster from those steep climbs and have more endurance mile after mile. A healthy heart is the foundation of life.

Exercises to Strengthen Your Heart

- Any exercise that raises your heart rate
- Lifting weights
- Steady-state cardio: all variations
- High-intensity interval training (HIIT) circuits
- Hiking
- A healthy diet

Now for drama's sake, I'm going to end this section with arguably the most important "muscle" needed for high performance on the trail . . .

Brain

Yes, I know the brain is technically an organ, not a muscle, but it's important nonetheless and worth mentioning. In fact, I believe it's so important for hiking success that I dedicate an entire chapter to this part of the equation later in the book.

What It Does: It's what gets you to the finish line when things get hard. It's where resilience and grit come from because it's absolutely going to get hard out there. Hiking rejuvenates our souls, but that doesn't mean it isn't hard. The most fulfilling adventures are usually the hard ones that you persevered through. It's not surprising that they're also the ones you tell the most stories about.

Why Your Brain Is Important on the Trail: Remember your muscles can be strong but it's your mind that's going to power you through the hard, wet, cold, unenjoyable days with endless ascents where you just feel like quitting. Don't underestimate the importance of mental toughness and grit when it comes to backcountry success. That all happens in your brain. So your brain gets an "honorable mention" here because it is the "muscle" (organ) that will often determine whether you keep going or give up. More on that later though . . .

Exercises to Strengthen Your Brain

- Train hard and challenge yourself regularly
- Train on the days you "don't feel like it"
- Train on the days you think you're "too busy"
- Train on the days you "don't feel motivated"

Forming the mental toughness, grit, and resilience needed for success on the trail happens when you voluntarily do hard things over and over again. That's how you learn to persevere when life gets hard. Remember, when you sign in at the trailhead you're choosing to do hard things in tough, rugged, uncomfortable locations and weather conditions. The more you show up for yourself and voluntarily do hard things on purpose (that is, training in the gym, hiking, etc.), the more you'll build this exact grit. When you show up for yourself day after day and do the work regardless of your emotions, your mind becomes stronger.

Now I want you to think back to your own hiking trips and reflect on what your limiting factors were.

Was your leg strength lacking?
Was endurance in your quads an issue?
Is your upper body weak?
Is your heart conditioning always a struggle?

Dumbbell incline bench press. Hikers need strong upper bodies too.

Squat. A full-body strength builder.

Did you have back pain from wearing your backpack?
All of the above?

Everybody has different areas they need to strengthen, so reflect on what areas need extra attention so you know what to focus on.

Now that you understand when, where, and how each muscle group comes into play on the trail, along with some exercises that can strengthen them, we can start putting together a training strategy. In the next section I'll show you how the Mountain-Strength Method looks in action with a blueprint of each training day. So take a sip of water, strap on your backpack, and let's keep going.

Mountain-Strength Method Part 1: Mountain-Strength Days: Building Foundational Strength

You can't out-cardio your way to the summit if your body isn't strong enough to take you there. In order to get strong you have to do the movements that get you strong. Here's how to build this foundational strength, what exercises to do, the sets and rep ranges, and how to structure these days in the gym so you reap the rewards on the trail.

Mountain-Strength Day Goal:
To build a strong foundation based on pure strength. These will be your hardest training days but also the most impactful on your overall hiking ability and fitness level.

Recommendation: 2 to 3 days per week

The Mountain-Strength Day Blueprint:
Each Mountain-Strength training session is broken down into four blocks:

1. Strength Block
2. "Elevation" Circuit
3. Trail Conditioning
4. Core Finisher

Warm-Up

It's always important to get your body warmed up before training. The goal of your warm-up is to prepare your muscles and joints for lifting, prevent injury, and elevate your heart rate. Always take a few minutes to get your body warm.

James's Favorite Warm-Up Exercises

- Jumping jacks x 50 reps
- 2-minute fast walk
- Hip and shoulder mobility movements

BLOCK 1: Strength Block

The strength block is where you're going to build strength and power, which will translate to a higher output on the trail. You aren't just strengthening your muscles either but also your bones, ligaments, tendons, and joints too. Heavy training will lower your chances of injury on the trail as well because heavy lifting increases your bone density and makes your body more resilient.

Whether your goal is backpacking or playing football, the foundation of your training program should be building strength. This is where that big, scary phrase from earlier comes into play: progressive overload. Take as much rest as you need between sets during this first block so you're fully recovered and ready to give 100 percent into your next set.

"How Much Weight Should I Lift?"

The weight should feel heavy and challenging for the amount of reps. Finding the correct weights for the prescribed rep range usually involves a few "warm-up sets" to ramp up to the weight you'll use for your "working sets." For example, if a program says, "3 sets of 8 reps" (3x8), those three sets are the "working sets," excluding warm-ups. Sometimes all three working sets will be at the same weight, sometimes they won't, but all three sets should challenge you for eight reps. Ideally your weight should be in that one to two RIR range we discussed earlier and each week aim to do a little more.

Types of Movements

Compound Movements: These are exercises that engage multiple muscles and joints in a single movement. I prefer compound movements when possible because they offer the most bang for your buck as they require a near full body effort.

Examples include barbell squats, deadlifts, bench press, and overhead press. Any variation of each will work well for our needs.

BLOCK 2: Elevation Circuits

After the strength portion of your workout you'll move on to the next part of your training session, Block 2: Elevation Circuits. My training/hiking partner and I refer to these circuits as "elevation circuits" because they're reminiscent of how hard your body works during steep climbs where you put your head down and grind your way through them one step at a time. These circuits build up your muscular strength *and* conditioning simultaneously. Hiking requires extended periods of heavy breathing with burning muscles, and these circuits aim to replicate the exact same physical demand of a steep climb.

Elevation circuits are not meant to be sprints though. Instead I want you to move at a challenging yet maintainable pace through the circuit. With an elevated heart rate you'll experience short bursts of high-energy outputs during each exercise. Think of a topographic map where the trail gains elevation, followed by a flat section, then onto more elevation gain. These circuits are implementing that same concept. Hard work, followed by a short break, followed by more hard work.

How to Complete:

1. Perform the first exercise.
2. Walk to the next exercise, take 1 to 2 deep breaths. Around 20 seconds between sets.
3. Complete the next exercise.
4. Repeat until the full circuit is complete.

Hiking isn't a sprint and neither are these. So find that steady, challenging, maintainable pace and go.

"How Much Weight Should I Lift?"

The weights will generally be moderate because you'll be doing a lot of work in a short period of time while breathing heavily with minimal rest. The weights don't need to be maximal, but you should aim to challenge yourself with each set. The goal is to do hard work while breathing heavily just like you will do on a steep ascent in the mountains.

Types of Movements

Upper and lower body movements of all kinds. Dumbbell, barbell, machine, and bodyweight movements. This circuit is your accessory* training but with a trail twist. I also highly recommend including at least one single-leg movement in each circuit.

*Note: Accessory movements are typically single-muscle exercises that target weaker muscles with the goal of strengthening your weak points.

BLOCK 3: Trail Conditioning

The trail conditioning portion is specifically designed to replicate the cardiovascular demands of hiking. This portion of the Mountain-Strength Day training session will train both your trail muscles and your heart in an athletic way. These exercises should be completed in one unbroken set *without* rest. Even if the pace is slow, find and maintain that steady pace just like you do on the trail.

Remember our goal with this training session is full-body strength that translates to a higher performance on the trail.

"How Much Weight Should I Lift?"

The goal here is to challenge yourself and maintain a pace. The harder you work in the gym, the easier the mountains will become. This portion of training will be around five to ten minutes in length and will vary in reps.

Types of Movements

- Step-ups wearing a loaded backpack
- Lunges wearing a loaded backpack
- Burpees
- Weighted carries
- Devil's presses
- Dumbbell snatches

BLOCK 4: Core Finisher

The core finisher at the end of your workout will strengthen your core stability. The goal is to improve your ability to carry a loaded backpack. A strong core will make every adventure more enjoyable because nobody wants back pain after hiking.

"How Much Weight Should I Lift?"

Bodyweight is often sufficient here; however, if you're advanced and want to wear a loaded backpack on some movements you can progressively overload the weight in your backpack to generate fantastic newfound core strength. The goal is to build up to multiple sets of multiple minutes of exercises like planks, bird dogs, and so on. If you're doing farmer's/weighted carries, however, aim to carry a heavy and challenging weight that tests your core stability as well as your overall strength and conditioning.

Types of Movements

- Planks
- Side planks
- Elevated planks
- Deadbugs
- Bird dogs
- Farmer's carry
- Weighted carry

Planks. A great way to build a bulletproof core.

"Mountain-Strength Day" Full Example

1. **Strength Block (30 Minutes)**
   Goal: Building strength, power, and muscle
   How: Pick 1 to 2 compound movements or variations
   - **Primary Lift:** 3 to 4 sets each in the 5 to 10 rep range aiming for 1 to 2 RIR
   - Progress weight or reps weekly
   - Examples:
     - Squat, trap bar deadlift, or leg press machine
     - Bench press or overhead press
2. **Elevation Circuit (15 Minutes)**
   Goal: Build strength, muscular endurance, and anaerobic conditioning
   How: A 3-exercise dumbbell/bodyweight/machine circuit at a consistent pace
   Example Circuit:
   - **3 to 4 Rounds:** Complete circuit wearing a loaded backpack:
     - Dumbbell lunges (10 reps per leg)
     - Dumbbell shoulder press (10 reps)
     - Dumbbell goblet squats (12 reps)
3. **Trail Conditioning (5 to 10 Minutes)**
   Goal: Build functional trail conditioning
   How: Pick 1 exercise and complete in one steady set with minimal rest
   Examples:
   - Weighted step-ups (onto a bench or box) holding dumbbells or wearing a loaded backpack x 50 reps per leg
   - Burpees x 30 reps
   - Weighted carries 4 rounds x 50 yards
4. **Core Finisher (2 to 5 Minutes)**
   Goal: Increase core stability for carrying a backpack
   How: Pick 1 exercise for 1 to 3 total minutes
   Examples:
   - Planks, all variations
   - Deadbugs
   - Mountain climbers
   - Bird dogs
   - Farmer's carry

Postworkout Mobility
Goal: Mobility work to aid recovery
How: Spend 2 to 5 minutes postworkout on mobility and recovery

Examples:
- Foam rolling
- Stretching
- Mobility

Mountain-Strength Day Training Principles
1. **Lift Heavy, Hike Hard**
   - Focus on compound, multijoint lifts that build total-body strength.
   - The weights should always challenge you for the rep range, typically leaving one to two "reps in reserve" (RIR) each working set.
2. **Progressive Overload**
   - Gradually increase weight or reps each week to force your muscles to adapt and grow.
   - Prioritize proper form, full range of motion, and the muscles doing the work.
3. **Functional Movements**
   - Strategically choose exercises that translate to your performance on the trail.
4. **Strength and Endurance Blends**
   - Replicate the muscular and cardiovascular demands of hiking.
   - Anaerobic and aerobic conditioning

Real-Trail Application

A strong foundation is the key to anything. When it comes to the trail, your legs will handle steeper climbs more efficiently, your lungs will be better equipped for the long miles, your backpack will feel lighter, and your body will be stronger top to bottom. Overall your performance on the trail will reach new heights as your adventures become even more fulfilling all around.

Mindset for Mountain-Strength Days

These days will require you to push yourself more than any other days. You're building mental toughness and the ability to keep going when it's hard as much as you're building physical strength. You'll have to do the same things on those long, hard, wet days on the trail too. Good thing you'll already be physically and mentally prepared to persevere.

Speaking of persevering, next I'll break down the day's designed to help you maneuver backcountry terrain and get through those big elevation gains, aptly named "Elevation Days."

MOUNTAIN-STRENGTH METHOD PART 2: ELEVATION DAYS: ATHLETICISM FOR THE BACKCOUNTRY
    athleticism: *noun.*
    athletic ability: the combination of qualities such as speed, strength, and
        agility that are characteristic of an athlete.
    (*Merriam-Webster Dictionary*)

At first glance hiking may not seem like an athletic endeavor, and if the majority of one's hiking experience comes from gentle nature walks, it's probably not. Once you're climbing mountains and backpacking rugged trails, however, it certainly becomes one. Having the ability to move like an athlete will dramatically improve your performance and confidence, so it's important to train like an athlete if we want to move like one. And what better way to build athleticism than by moving your entire body with just your body, right?

Remember, you're a mountain athlete now—time to train like one.

Mountain climbers. The name says it all. Great movement for hikers.

Elevation Day Goal:
To build athleticism (strength, speed, and agility) and the anaerobic conditioning needed to tackle heavy elevation gains and maneuver the backcountry like an athlete.

Recommendation: 1 to 2 days per week

The Blueprint
Elevation days train your upper and lower body through the use of bodyweight training circuits to improve your strength, speed, endurance, and agility. Circuits can vary and getting creative makes them more fun.

Time Duration: 15 to 45 minutes

Some circuits may include things like . . .

Every Minute on the Minute (EMOM): Perform the circuit and then rest for the remainder of each minute. Begin the next round at the top of every minute. This will create incentive to work hard to complete the exercises as fast as possible so you get more rest time each minute.

As Many Rounds as Possible (AMRAP): Cycle through the exercises one after the other and complete as many rounds as possible in the given time. This creates incentive to work hard to see how many rounds you can complete. This is a great option when you're short on time. Pick a few movements and rep ranges, set a timer, and get to work. Remember, ten minutes is better than zero minutes. This will ensure you make those ten minutes count.

Tabatas: A tabata is broken down into mini-sets consisting of twenty seconds of work and ten seconds of rest. Perform one movement for eight rounds of the twenty seconds on/ten seconds rest for a total of four minutes. Then pick another exercise and repeat. Tabatas are another powerful technique to get a lot of work completed in a short period of time.

Ladders: Do each exercise of the circuit for ten reps, then each exercise for nine reps, then for eight reps, and so on, all the way down to one rep. Then reverse the ladder back up to ten reps of each exercise.

Elevation Day Examples
Example 1
4 Rounds
- Skater jumps x 10 reps (per leg)
- Mountain climbers x 20 seconds
- Bodyweight squats x 20 reps
- Mountain climbers x 20 seconds
- Push-ups x 10 reps
- Mountain climbers x 20 seconds
- Burpees x 5 reps
- Jumping jacks x 30 reps
- Rest 60 seconds

Example 2
As Many Rounds as Possible (AMRAP)
Warm-up: 50 jumping jacks
As many rounds as possible (AMRAP) in 20 minutes

- 5 burpees
- 10 jump squats
- 20 mountain climbers
- 30-second wall sit

Note: Modify the movements if needed (that is, burpees without push-ups or jumps, elevated push-ups against a counter, etc.). What matters most is putting in your best effort, challenging yourself, and getting the work accomplished.

Example 3
3 Tabatas
Rest 2 minutes between each tabata

1. Burpees
2. Reverse lunges
3. Mountain climbers

Example 4
Ladder 10 - 1 - 10

- Jumping jacks
- Jump squats
- Push-ups
- Mountain climbers

Training Principles

1. **High Intensity Interval Training (HIIT)**
   - HIIT training has you work hard, then rest, then work hard, then rest. This mimics the cardiovascular demands of the ever-changing terrain on the trail.
   - To prepare you for steep elevation gains with burning legs and lungs.
2. **Muscular Endurance**
   - To build muscular, joint, and cardiovascular endurance using just your bodyweight.
   - Full body, upper body, and lower body movements.
3. **Speed**
   - To improve your muscles', heart's, and lungs' ability to recover quicker between climbs.
   - To increase your ability to move fast on the trail.
4. **Agility**
   - To prepare your body for quick, sudden movements on the trail.
   - To improve your ability to confidently maneuver your body over backcountry terrain.

Real-Trail Application

The elevation days will help you from the trailhead to the summit. Due to the interval training your muscles and heart rate will recover quicker during steep ascents, and the bodyweight movements will improve your agility maneuvering varied terrain. Having that improved agility will also dramatically decrease your risk of injury on the trail.

    Bottom line: Your athleticism (speed, strength, and agility) will improve all around.

The Ascent: Strength Training for Stronger Hiking

Bodyweight squats. The more squats the better.

Mindset for Elevation Days

Just because these days utilize bodyweight training does not mean they'll be "easy." Bodyweight training forces you to move athletically, and these days are often the hardest for people, especially if you haven't trained for a while. Prepare your mind to go hard and fast in a short period of time. This type of fitness will generate the ability to endure long days with big elevation gains. So push yourself and give it your all. You'll be glad you did when your heart is no longer beating through your chest on every climb.

Now that we've started building foundational strength, followed by a

Guiding a winter hike in the Adirondack High Peaks. −30°. Wright Peak.

mix of strength and conditioning, let's create that long-distance endurance. Time to train the heart to handle long miles. Let's talk about approach days.

Mountain-Strength Method Part 3: Approach Days: Endurance Training for Long Miles

I've been asked this question a hundred times by both new and experienced hikers:

"What is the right hiking pace?"

Like most things in life, the answer is "it depends." However, I do believe there is a pace that scales to each person's ability and gives them the best chance for success.

Stair climber wearing a loaded backpack. Great hiking endurance builder.

Answer:
Hike as fast as you can but as slow as you need to go so that you never have to stop.

Finding this sweet spot, as slow as it may be, is going to be the right pace for you. It's the age-old "tortoise and the hare" story: Slow and *steady* wins the race. This steady pace ensures you're always moving forward, and that's the pace to hike. Whether that's a mile an hour or three miles an hour, it doesn't matter. Stops always eat up more time than we think they do, and they stop the flow. Finding that steady, maintainable pace keeps us in the groove moving forward.

Hiking and backpacking are long-distance sports, and we'll give ourselves the best chance for success by building a strong body top to bottom and also by being well conditioned. The trail will demand the ability to move with an elevated heart rate over a long period of time, and the approach days prepare us for that demand.

Where I live here in the Adirondack Mountains, most mountains have a long five-plus-mile approach just to get to the base of the peak before climbing. These approaches are the mountain's version of steady-state cardio. So far we've focused on getting our muscles and joints strong, now let's focus on getting our heart and lungs strong too.

Approach Day Goal:
To build endurance and the ability to maintain an elevated heart rate over the course of many miles.

Recommendation: 1 to 2 days per week for 30 to 60 minutes a session. Aim for zones 2 or 3 heart rate.

The Blueprint

- 30 to 60 total minutes
- Choose 1 or 2 different exercises for the workout (run, fast walk, elliptical, bike, rower, stair climber, hiking, rucking, etc.)
- Maintain your pace and heart rate in zone 2 or 3

Approach Day Examples

Complete forty minutes of steady state cardio of your choice.

Choose from running, bicycling, swimming, fast walking, elliptical machine, stair climber, rucking, treadmill with incline, rower, and so on.

Find a good pace with an elevated heart rate and maintain that pace for the duration of the training session. If preferred, you can split it up by doing two different exercises for twenty minutes each.

Training Principles

1. **Steady-State Cardio (Aerobic)**
   - Conditioning your heart muscle for long miles and steep climbs.
2. **Zones 2 to 3 Heart Rate**
   - Zone 2: A moderate-intensity exercise level maintain-

Running. It's a good way to build endurance but shouldn't be the foundation of your training.

ing your heart rate between 60 and 70 percent of your maximum heart rate. A "conversational pace" where you can comfortably talk while exercising.
- Zone 3: A moderately high-intensity exercise level maintaining your heart rate between 70 to 80 percent of your maximum heart rate. A level where you can still maintain a conversation but with more effort and heavier breathing.

3. **Challenging but Maintainable Pace**
   - Find a challenging pace and maintain it for the duration of the training session.
   - Aim for a minimum thirty minutes per session.

Enjoying a winter day above the clouds in the Adirondack High Peaks.

Real-Trail Application

Hiking is a miles game, and the more prepared we are to tackle those miles the better off we'll be. Conditioning always comes into play during short, steep climbs, as well as your overall endurance for the hike. Mixed with the strength days you'll find your muscles and heart are all conditioned, which will lead to great days on the trail.

Mindset for Approach Days

I want you to think of your approach days (aka cardio day) as the "heart training" day. Just like we do biceps curls to build our biceps muscles, we do cardio to build our heart muscle.

Lifting heavy weights and completing HIIT circuits train your heart too (and muscles), but they do it in a different way. The approach day focuses specifically on heart health and increasing your aerobic capacity. This will help you build confidence in your ability to handle long miles in the backcountry moving at a steady and consistent pace all day long.

Mountain-Strength Method Part 4: Backpack Days: Building Backpack Strength for Hiking

Do you ever come back from a long hike and your back is shot from wearing the pack? It's not unusual because when in life do you wear a fully loaded backpack for hours and miles on end besides for hiking? Pretty much never, right?

Backpack strength is often a hiker's "Achilles's heel" because it's innocently forgotten. Your ability to carry a heavy pack is a major factor in still feeling strong at the end of a hike, let alone at the trailhead. We'll build this strength by rucking or by actually going hiking. Time on your feet while wearing a loaded pack is key. So whether you're pounding the pavement in your neighborhood or hitting your local trails, just load your pack and start walking.

Backpack Day Goal:
To build your strength carrying a loaded backpack and accumulate miles on your feet.

Recommendation: 1 to 2 days per week for 30 to 60 minutes a session. Your backpack should weigh more than your fully loaded hiking pack.

The Blueprint

- 30 to 60 total minutes
- Wear a loaded backpack heavier than your hiking pack
- Walk fast

Backpack Day Examples

Forty-five minute ruck wearing a loaded backpack on varied terrain (if possible)
Backpack weight: Twenty to forty pounds
Goal distance: 2.3 miles

Training Principles

1. **Heavy Backpack**
    - Load your pack heavier than your typical hiking pack so your pack on the trail feels light.

2. **Miles and Speed**
   - Push yourself with both the mileage and the speed with which you're walking, especially if walking on flat ground.
   - Aim for a minimum of two miles or thirty minutes.
3. **Progressive Overload**
   - Add backpack weight each week.
   - Increase your mileage and/or duration each week.
4. **Active Recovery**
   - Rucks are generally a low-stress training day and serve triple duty as an active recovery day as well as building backpack strength and improving your trail endurance

Ruck. A great way to get time on your feet wearing a loaded backpack whether it's walking in the woods or your neighborhood.

Real-Trail Application

Being able to confidently carry your heavy backpack speaks for itself. An extra pound or two in your backpack doesn't matter when you're strong. Sorry "ultralighters," but that's the reality. It's economical to be strong.

Mindset for Backpack Days

This day can be completed on the trail or in your neighborhood and should be thought of as your "practice" day. If you're playing football, for example, you'll train in the weight room and then on the field. This is your "on the field" day. When possible, just go hiking.

COMMON MISTAKES HIKERS MAKE WHEN STRENGTH TRAINING
1. **Skipping Upper Body Days:** Hiking may be a leg-dominant activity, but your upper body should be strong too so you can maneuver your own body. It's a full-body sport and just like your legs, your upper body helps propel you up the mountain too, but in different ways. So don't focus solely on leg strength because being strong top to bottom is always better.

2. **Endless Cardio:** The never-ending cycle of endless cardio may get your heart strong, but it isn't going to get your muscles strong. In fact, it will have the opposite effect because it will typically cause you to lose muscle mass. You need that muscle to power your way up the mountain. Cardio is needed, of course, but it should not be the foundation of your training if you want to have stronger mountain adventures.

James finishing up the Northville-Placid Trail. What a great feeling and adventure.

3. **Training Too Light:** Lifting light weights for twenty-five reps won't prepare you for a heavy pack and long, steep miles. The weights you're lifting should always challenge you and get you stronger. I've found lifting moderate/heavy weights for sets in the five to ten rep range is generally the sweet spot.
4. **Ignoring Core and "Backpack Strength":** When you're carrying a loaded backpack for hours and miles on end it's crucial to have a strong core to handle the load. Plus, you're carrying it over uneven terrain and climbing elevation. The best way to prepare for this demand is by strengthening your core and getting miles on your feet while wearing the loaded backpack.
5. **No Progressive Overload:** Lifting the same weights or running the exact same distance over and over will not generate growth. Your body needs a reason to adapt and grow so give it a reason by progressively overloading your training.
6. **Neglecting Nutrition and Recovery:** Muscles grow when you sleep and need the proper nutrition to grow. Without each you're just breaking your body down as opposed to breaking it down *and* rebuilding it stronger. Your nutrition and recovery protocol should support your goals.

START TRAINING, KEEP READING

Now that you know the strategy behind the Mountain-Strength Method I want you to start training as you continue reading through the book. There's no time like the present, right? Like the old saying goes, the best time to plant a tree was twenty years ago and the next best time is now. So flip to chapter 6 and pick the training program that works best for you and get to work. There are several options to choose from based on your preferences.

Training is only one part of the equation on this journey though, so keep reading, but I also want you to **start training now**.

Training Should Be Hard Because Climbing Mountains Is Hard Too

Climbing mountains is hard. Backpacking long miles in the woods across rugged terrain is hard. Therefore, in order to prepare properly we need to simulate that same "hard" when it comes to our training effort. We need to push ourselves every time we hit the gym or pound the pavement. To generate growth your body must be forced into it. That's life though, right? Those hard times we all go through, while difficult in the moment, are also the exact times we experience the most personal growth too. Training is no different. So whether you want to get stronger, lose weight, burn fat, build muscle, or train for a sport, you have to kick it up a notch to that next level in order to generate growth. That "next level" is also going to look different for every person. When you're honest with yourself, though, you'll know whether you're

Leg press. A great machine to build strong legs, knees, ankles, and lungs.

truly giving it your all or if you're letting yourself off the hook with your effort. Effort is free and a 100 percent effort looks the same for everyone. The output of weights, reps, or speed might look different, but the effort itself remains the same. Full effort is full effort.

Staying within your comfort zone, rarely elevating your heart rate, avoiding lifting heavy things, or never taking your muscles near failure will unfortunately keep you exactly where you are now, aka status quo. It's up to you to facilitate growth in the gym the same way it's up to you to get yourself to the next summit. No one can do the work for you, and it falls solely on you and your effort. It should be an empowering feeling knowing you have the power to control how well you perform in the backcountry. I have no doubts you are going to give it your all and rise to the occasion.

James hiking in the Adirondacks on a flawless summer day.

When it's all said and done the mountains are going to have no problem pushing you. So let's beat them to the punch by preparing for that every time we step into the gym. I challenge you to give a 110 percent effort every training session. Some days you'll have more to give than other days, but giving your best effort for that day is what counts. The next time you step onto the trail you'll be glad you pushed yourself beforehand because you will be prepped, primed, and prepared to be pushed by the mountains.

"I'm Not as Broken as I Think I Am"
*When injured, always consult your doctor first.

Over my lifetime of training I've had my fair share of tweaks, twinges, pops, and injuries, from minor achy joints to full blown lower back tweaks and multiple bouts of physical therapy for shoulder pain. However there is one consistent lesson I've learned from all of them. I want you to grab a highlighter and highlight this next sentence:

"I'm not as broken as I think I am."

The next time you feel a tweak or twinge in the gym, I want you to take a deep breath and repeat that sentence to yourself over and over again . . . and then again for good measure. It will dramatically improve how your mind responds to it.

Our mind is powerful. When we quickly remind ourselves "we're not broken," our ability to persevere despite setbacks improves dramatically. How often in your own life have you tweaked your back or had an achy knee or shoulder and said to yourself, "Now I guess I can't do *anything*" and then you threw in the towel all together? We've all been there, me included. Instead, had you focused on what you *can* do instead of what you *can't* do, you could have continued making progress, trained around the injury, and learned that same lesson I did.

For example, let's say you feel shoulder pain overhead pressing. Ask yourself, "What *doesn't* hurt? What *can* I do instead?" and proceed to hammer those movements and muscle groups. Maybe you can't shoulder press for a while but you can bench press, or maybe you can't do any pressing but you can do triceps extensions, back exercises, and lower body exercises pain free. Great. Train those movements hard. Maybe you tweaked your lower back and it seems like you can't do anything because even standing up and walking is hard. Well, your arms still work don't they? Train your arms. Maybe squatting with a barbell hurts but you can do slow and controlled bodyweight to keep the area warm and moving. See how this works? **It's a perspective shift.** It's training your mind to focus on what you can control and not what you can't. You may not be able to control the fact that you feel pain now, but you can control how you respond to it. Perseverance is a choice and it's learned through practice.

The faster you adopt this mindset, the faster you're going to learn just how "*not broken*" you are and how strong your mind and body truly are. Injury, though difficult and annoying, is a great time to get the mental reps in building perseverance and powering forward even when it's hard and uncomfortable. This perseverance will bode well for you when it gets hard

The Ascent: Strength Training for Stronger Hiking

out on the trail. And it's going to get hard out there too. Good thing you'll already be physically and mentally prepared to tackle that "hard."

Now grab that highlighter again and highlight this next sentence too:

"Anything beats nothing."

Any training is better than no training. Doing just two exercises is better than doing zero exercises. Training hard for eight minutes on your lunch break is better than zero minutes. Always. This mentality is not only going to improve your training and progress, it's also going to infiltrate how you approach challenges and hard things in everyday life too. It's amazing how much fitness prepares us for the real world.

Heading down the backside of New York's tallest peak, Mt. Marcy, on our way to Mt. Skylight.

The first two steps of the "I'm Not as Broken as I Think I Am" protocol are mental, but the third step is physical. It can be summed up in three words. Grab that highlighter . . .

"Movement is medicine."

Remind yourself that movement is medicine. Get that blood flowing any way you can because blood delivers nutrients and oxygen to the injured areas in your body.

Our bodies are so strong that it's astonishing. It takes learning these lessons to realize that for yourself. So the next time you feel that tweak or twinge, remind yourself of those three highlighted sentences. It will be a mental and physical gamechanger to help you pivot so you keep moving forward despite the setback. And yes, sometimes it's difficult choosing to carry yourself in this manner and adopt this "overcome" mentality when things look bleak, but this mentality will serve you well every time. I guarantee it.

"I.N.A.B.A.I.T.I.A." Protocol
Repeat steps 1 to 3 for 3 sets of 5 reps.

1. "I'm not as broken as I think I am" x 5 reps
2. "Anything beats nothing" x 5 reps
3. "Movement is medicine" x 5 reps

Next Steps: Strength Is Your Trail Superpower

Hiking isn't supposed to be easy, but it doesn't have to be painfully hard either. Whether you're navigating difficult terrain in the backcountry or in the challenges of life, strength is always a superpower. I'm not just talking physically either because your mental strength is equally important, but we'll get to that later in the book.

The long miles and steep climbs will challenge your body and your mind, but by strategically strengthening your muscles, joints, lungs and heart your performance will elevate like never before. Those soul-crushing days on the trail are going to be a thing of the past.

Every time you pick up a dumbbell, do a squat, or go for a ruck you're investing in yourself and your backcountry adventures. You're building sweat equity that will pay off the moment you step onto the trail feeling strong, confident, and prepared for whatever the great outdoors throws your way.

Overhead press. Strong shoulders are a must for life.

YOUR ASSIGNMENT

Now that you've learned this battle-tested training formula for hiking, here's your homework:

1. **Commit to yourself and make training a nonnegotiable in your life.**
   Prioritize your physical fitness daily. Remember every time you show up to train, rain or shine, you're showing up for yourself. This extends way beyond simply training for hiking.
2. **Plan out your training.**
   Just like studying your map or prepping your gear, planning your weekly training days in advance gives you the best odds for success. It teaches you how to persevere when life or the trail throw you a curveball. Good thing you'll be prepared to still swing the bat anyways.
3. **Keep showing up.**
   The mountains are going to test your grit like no other, but you can build that grit in the gym by showing up week after week regardless of time, schedule, emotions, or excuses. We all have reasons not to train, but when we rise above those excuses and remind ourselves why we're doing this, it becomes easier to keep showing up for ourselves. When in doubt revisit Step #1.

Farmer's carry. One of my all-time favorite exercises. When you carry the weight in the woods sometimes you even need the snowshoes in the Adirondacks.

Now that you've learned how to break down your muscles it's time to discuss how to rebuild them so they grow bigger and stronger.

Let's continue up the mountain and dive into nutrition, hydration, and recovery—on and off the trail.

CHAPTER 4

The Refuel: Nutrition, Hydration, and Recovery

IN HIKING, *REFUELING* MEANS GIVING YOUR BODY THE NUTRITION AND hydration it needs to keep going strong. Just like your car needs gas for a long drive, your body needs fuel to power through long miles and elevation gains. Whether it's a snack on the trail, a solid meal after a hike, or staying on top of your water and electrolytes, refueling properly is critical to keep your energy up, your legs moving, and your mind sharp out there.

Hiking on Empty in the Adirondack High Peaks
It was a subzero winter day deep in the Adirondack High Peaks when both of my legs cramped up so badly I couldn't bend them anymore. I was hiking with some friends climbing the Lower Great Range. We had six summits on tap for the day and we were aiming to be on our second summit for the sunrise. Given this itinerary, we started dark and early that day as usual.

The hike began with a three-mile approach to the base of the first peak before beginning to climb the 2,100 feet of elevation over a couple miles to the summit. After a couple hours of crunching through the snow and breaking trail, we made it to the top of our first peak of the day: Sawteeth Mountain, standing just over 4,100 feet elevation in the pitch black Adirondack sky. The white snow on the mountains reflected the moonlight glow in a way only the mountains can. Throughout the climb up Sawteeth, however, I only took sips of water periodically and didn't eat anything. After all who wants to eat or drink when you're hiking in the middle of the night when it's below zero degrees, right? Bad choice.

After layering up and enjoying the High Peak summit in the dead of night we started back down Sawteeth to the range trail to continue our trek across the Lower Great Range. Pyramid Peak was up next. This involved a quick 900 feet of elevation gain in just over half a mile. Our crew had to break trail so our legs, lungs, and snowshoes were working overtime that morning. Then just over half way up Pyramid, as I dug my snowshoe into the snow-covered trail, it happened. My entire quad muscle cramped and locked up. Then my other leg followed suit. From my hips all the way down to my ankles. Everything locked and it was painful. My legs decided they were straight up out of gas thanks to my neglect fueling them. So there I was, frustrated, cold, and six miles deep in the Adirondack backcountry, in the dead of winter, on top of a High Peak, and I was so dehydrated I couldn't bend my legs.

Immediately I dropped my pack and started drinking large amounts of electrolyte water, ate salty snacks, and ate a banana for some added potassium. The entire climb up Pyramid Peak I had to take light, gingerly steps to keep more cramps at bay; however, the damage had already been done. Once dehydration sets in it's hard to recover from it. That's why it's better to not let it happen in the first place. I was not smart that day.

I contemplated abandoning ship and heading down the mountain solo, but I pressed on slowly to Pyramid with the crew, where I refueled with a substantial amount of food and electrolytes on the summit. It took hours to fully recover, but after many more bouts of cramps and summiting our third peak for the day, Gothics, I was finally feeling normal again. Well, normalish. The anxiety of cramping up again ran through my head almost every step for the rest of the hike.

It's scary being deep in the mountains, miles from any road, in the middle of January, when your legs stop working properly. Things could have gone a lot worse that day, especially given the winter element, but I was fortunate to eventually recover from the dehydration and muscle cramps. However, all of this could have and should have been avoided altogether. I was not intentional or disciplined enough with my nutrition like usual, and I paid the price. After all, my body was working overtime just to stay warm, let alone the hiking;

A frozen beard kind of day on Tabletop Mountain.

therefore, it was even more important to ensure I was fueling appropriately for the climb. Nutrition on the trail is critical for success and should be aligned with our goals. My goal was to summit six mountains that day so I should have fueled like it. More lessons learned courtesy of the mountains.

Nutrition for Training and Life
Nutrition Is Fuel

Nutrition is fuel and it's vital for success whether you're trying to perform better on the trail, lose weight, build muscle, or want general health. In this section we're going to simplify nutrition and discuss how to eat for performance so your diet supports your training and hiking goals. By the end you'll have a well above average understanding of nutrition along with a strategy to implement for your training and the trail to set yourself up for success. Grab that highlighter once again and highlight this next sentence:

Food is fuel and it's your responsibility to fuel right.

Let's start with the king, the often misunderstood and drastically underconsumed foundation of any good nutrition plan: PROTEIN.

Protein: The Building Block of Strength

I'll cut right to the chase here so you understand why protein is so important. Protein helps you build muscle and maintain muscle when dieting, and it keeps you full longer. The goal in the gym is to break down your muscles so they rebuild bigger and stronger. When it comes to nutrition, your protein intake is the biggest contributing factor to whether those muscles will grow bigger and stronger. Without the proper protein intake you're just breaking your muscles down but not properly rebuilding them. That's a recipe for disaster, injury, and never reaching your goals. Think of the relationship between protein and training like offering someone constructive criticism. Usually you mention something positive first, then offer constructive criticism, followed by another positive note at the end. Breaking down your muscles without optimally rebuilding them is like only offering the criticism without the "constructive" part. At that point you're just criticizing someone and that helps no one, right? Similarly, breaking down your muscles without properly rebuilding them helps no one.

So it's time to eat your protein. But how much protein? I'm glad you asked.

How Much Protein Should I Eat?

The general consensus for protein intake within the world of fitness is **one gram of protein per pound of your goal bodyweight.**

If you weigh 200 pounds you should eat 200 grams of protein daily. If you weigh 200 pounds but you're trying to slim down to 150 pounds, then you should be eating a *minimum* of 150 grams of protein per day. Seven days a week.

This may seem "hard" at first, especially if you're coming from a low-protein diet like most of the population, but it's just about being strategic and intentional with your diet the same way you need to be strategic and intentional with your training to get results.

Note: If eating protein feels "hard," it may be time to look in the mirror and reevaluate your definition of "hard" before you get on the trail.

Metabolism and Muscle Mass

So far you've learned that protein helps you build and maintain muscle. That's important if we want to perform our best in the gym and on the trail, but its importance runs deeper than that. On top of the fact that it's better to be strong than weak, your muscle-to-fat ratio is one of the biggest contributors to your metabolism. I'm sure you're already aware, but if not, your metabolism is the process where your body converts food into energy. The higher your metabolism, the more calories your body burns at rest, meaning the more calories you can eat daily.

Many people think their metabolism "slows down" as they age. In reality, what typically happens is that people slow down and their metabolism follows suit. They stop doing hard things physically and often adopt a high-carb, highly processed, low-protein diet. So it's not that their metabolism chose to slow down because of their age, it's that *they* slowed down. As a result their muscle mass withered away so their metabolism decreased too. This often causes unwanted body fat because people's calorie intake usually stays the same—or goes up due to their highly processed diet—and their protein consumption and physical activity decrease. It's a true recipe for unwanted weight gain. Your body essentially went through a recomposition in a bad way, trading away muscle for fat and a slower metabolism.

It doesn't have to be that way though.
Here are two ways to avoid these metabolism woes:

1. Eat a diet that supports muscle preservation.
   How? By eating a high-protein (one gram per pound of bodyweight) whole foods diet as much as possible.
2. Tell your body to *"keep the muscle, burn the fat."*
   How? Strength training. By lifting heavy things regularly you're reminding your body you need these muscles to survive.

Just like the cave men who came before us, our bodies are designed to survive the winter. Therefore our body will choose to hold onto body fat and shed that "unneeded" muscle mass first unless we remind it we need that muscle to survive. The best way to accomplish this is by eating that high-protein diet and regularly challenging your muscles. That muscle mass will ensure your metabolism burns hot, and your overall health and longevity will thank you. Plus you'll look better too, and who doesn't want that?

Good protein sources include

- meat (beef, chicken, turkey, pork, lamb, bison, venison, elk, etc.),
- fish and shellfish,
- eggs,
- dairy (Greek yogurt, cheese, cottage cheese), and
- beans (if your stomach tolerates them).

Note: Just because something *has* protein in it doesn't necessarily make it a "protein source." Whenever possible, choose protein sources that have *at least* ten grams of protein per one hundred calories. That's a good rule of thumb for snacks too.

How Protein Impacts Hikers

Eating a high-protein diet may seem like an impossible task when you're backpacking. However it's entirely possible it just requires more effort but will be worth the reward. Most backpackers go heavy on processed carbs and fats but neglect protein. Keeping your protein level high will improve your muscle recovery day to day, which will result in stronger, longer miles on the trail. It will also help you fend off muscle loss dramatically, which will keep your body performing at its highest level. We'll get into this more later in the book with a high-protein shopping list for backpackers.

Key Takeaways About Protein

Muscle Repair and Growth

The primary function of protein is to facilitate muscle repair and growth following your workout or after a long day on the trail. Protein does this by providing the important amino acids needed for muscle growth (this is called "protein synthesis"). Muscle mass is a critical component for longevity and a strong, resilient body.

Improved Recovery

Consuming protein postworkout or posthike helps speed up the recovery process so you can train more frequently and with greater intensity. If you're on the trail, it prepares you for more miles tomorrow. Yes, I'm looking at you, backpackers!

Maintaining Muscle Mass

Adequate protein intake helps prevent muscle loss, especially when cutting calories or if you're backpacking for extended periods of time. The goal is always to burn fat, not muscle, right? This is partly why most backpackers lose their upper body muscles while backpacking. What a shame.

Metabolism

Your muscle-to-fat ratio mass is one of the biggest factors in your metabolism. The more muscle mass you have, the higher your metabolism will be. Protein (and strength training) helps you keep your hard-earned muscle mass and therefore enjoy a higher metabolism.

Daily Intake

Your daily intake should be one gram of protein per pound of your goal bodyweight. This involves being strategic and intentional with your nutrition.

Now that we've tackled protein, let's make sure your energy levels are high every time you train. Let's talk about carbs.

Carbohydrates: Your Primary Energy Source

Carbohydrates are your body's primary source for energy, particularly for high-intensity exercise like strength workouts.

Let's break down the process in a simple manner:

1. First you eat your carbs (rice, potatoes, bread, sugary snacks, etc.).
2. Those carbs are then broken down into energy (glucose) and stored in your liver and muscles (these are called "glycogen stores").
3. Now your body has the energy or "fuel" it needs to perform effectively while training or hiking.

In short, carbs provide energy. Think of your body as the car and carbs as the gasoline to make the engine run.

How Many Carbs Should I Eat?

This will vary for each person depending on your goals and needs. For example, if your goal is building muscle, you'll likely eat more carbs (and therefore more calories) than someone whose goal is burning fat and losing weight. A good place to start is by eating the same amount of carbs as protein and adjust from there based on your goals, results, energy, and performance level.

Note: As it pertains to weight loss, overall calories consumed must be lower than your calories burned. Calories are the most important factor for weight loss. So it's not that carbs hinder weight loss necessarily, it's just that lowering your carbs is an easy way to eat fewer calories.

Different Types of Carbs: Simple Versus Complex

What carbs are best, simple or complex? Well, they're both important and serve different roles. The main difference between simple and complex carbohydrates is how quickly they digest. Simple carbs are digested quickly, while complex carbs are digested more slowly.

Let's dive into some quick facts so you can learn which carb source is best for your needs.

Simple Carbs

What: Sugary snacks, energy gels, fruit juices, honey, maple syrup, candy, cereals, cookies, cakes, and so on.

Why: They digest quickly.
When: Great just before and/or during training, steep climbs, or any high-intensity activity.

Pros

- Digest quickly
- Provide quick bursts of energy
- Can quickly replenish glycogen stores (aka energy) during training/hiking

Cons

- Can lead to "sugar crash" later
- Generally less nutritious
- Lack fiber and many nutrients

Complex Carbs

What: Fruits, whole grains, pastas, potatoes, breads.
Why: Sustained energy throughout the day.
When: Your energy foundation usually eaten at meals.

Pros

- Provides sustained energy due to slower digestion
- High in fiber, which helps regulate blood sugar levels
- More filling and can help with weight management
- Typically contain more vitamins and minerals than simple carbs

Cons

- Take longer to digest potentially
- Generally less impactful for immediate energy needs

Training Carb Strategy

For your performance purposes in the gym, complex carbs (rice, potatoes, whole grains) should be your primary energy source eaten at meals, and then strategically eat simple carbs (sugary carbs) for quick energy needs just before/during your training.

What the Heck Is "Carb Timing"?

I'm a bottom line guy by nature so I don't typically sweat the small stuff. As long as you get the food in throughout the day you'll be just fine. However, because our goal is to get stronger and fitter for hiking from a performance level, it's worth noting carb timing. If you want the most optimal approach, generally the closer you eat your carbs around your workout or hike—roughly a couple hours before/after—the more energy you'll have to perform.

For example, if you eat fifty to one hundred grams of carbs a couple hours before your workout, you'll have more energy for your workout. More energetic workouts usually lead to better results. Then immediately following your workout, after you just depleted your muscles' energy, eating another fifty to one hundred grams of carbs will replenish the energy stores you just burned. This will ensure your muscles are ready to go again tomorrow. This is higher-level stuff, but it's worth mentioning because it can improve your overall performance in the gym and on the trail.

How Carbohydrates Impact Hikers

Carbs are paramount for your energy level for those long days on the trail. Many variables exist that can cause low energy, but oftentimes it comes down to the fact that you've burned out your energy stores. Carbs will help you refill your body with that much needed energy. Having a strategic nutrition plan on the trail means fueling with the right carbs at the right time so you hike better. When you're dragging, reach for something in the simple carbohydrates category, and then aim to refuel at your next meal with complex carbs. We'll do a deeper dive on this later in the book.

Key Takeaways About Carbohydrates

Carbs = Energy
Just like gasoline powers a car, carbohydrates fuel your body for hard training. Without enough, your body will run low on energy and your performance will suffer.

How Many Carbs Should You Eat?

Start by matching your carb intake to your protein intake and adjust based on your goals. More carbs = more energy (calories) for performance and muscle building. Fewer carbs = better for fat loss (less calories). Just be aware "more carbs" also means "more calories" too. Eat in alignment with your goals.

Simple Carbs Versus Complex Carbs

- **Simple Carbs** (honey, energy gels, sugary snacks) digest quickly and provide fast energy. Best eaten *before or during* high-intensity efforts like training, steep climbs, or long hikes.
- **Complex Carbs** (whole grains, potatoes, fruits) digest slower and provide sustained energy throughout the day. Best eaten *in meals* for steady energy levels.

Strategic Carb Timing

Eat simple carbs for quick energy boosts and complex carbs as your steady fuel source. Balancing both will lead to the best results in the gym and on the trail.

Healthy Fats: Bodily Function and Endurance Fuel

When it comes to nutrition for hiking, training, and overall performance, most people zero in on protein and carbohydrates for good reason. And while those are the key players, fats are often overlooked—or worse, demonized. The truth is that fats are essential for long-lasting energy and endurance, which makes them a vital part of a good trail nutrition strategy. They also help with recovery and general bodily function from your ability to absorb important vitamins to hormones to joint health. As you can see, fats deserve a seat at the table.

Let's quickly break down why fats matter and how to use them strategically in your nutrition plan to fuel your life and adventures.

How Much Fat Should You Eat?

Unlike protein and carbs, fat intake is a bit more flexible and depends on your personal energy needs. Fats are the most energy-dense macronutrient, sitting at nine calories per gram compared to four calories per gram like protein and carbs. On the trail that's high bang for your buck; off the trail, though, it can be a tough reality for my fellow peanut butter and cheese lovers who may be counting calories. It's easy to overeat calories with high fat content.

The higher calorie count of fats makes them quite valuable for long-duration activities like backpacking because fats take longer to digest, resulting in a more steady energy throughout the day.

If you're counting macros, a general rule of thumb is to aim for 0.3 to 0.5 grams of fat per pound of bodyweight per day. For example:

- A 150-pound hiker might aim for **45 to 75 grams of fat per day.**
- A 200-pound hiker might aim for **60 to 100 grams of fat per day.**

If you're training hard and hiking long distances, you may lean toward the higher end. If you're in a fat loss phase you should opt for lower calories, but never cut fats too much because your body needs them to function optimally. A well-functioning body is pretty important regardless of your goal, wouldn't you agree?

Note: Most people will find themselves getting adequate fats if they're hitting their protein needs with animal proteins (meat). When backpacking this may not always be easy, but in general life you may not need to dive too deep into fats if your protein comes mostly from meat and your calorie goals align.

Some Good Fats for Performance and Recovery

- Egg yolks
- Avocados
- Nuts (almonds, walnuts, cashews, macadamia)
- Nut butters (peanut butter, almond butter, cashew butter)
- Seeds (chia, flax, pumpkin, hemp)
- Fatty fish (salmon, sardines, mackerel, tuna)
- Coconut oil
- Olive oil
- Dark chocolate (85 percent or higher)
- Meat

Fats to Avoid or Minimize

- Processed seed oils (soybean, corn, canola, vegetable, grapeseed, etc.)
- Fried foods and fast food
- Highly processed snacks

How Fats Impact Hiking and Training

Because fats offer long-lasting energy, they're an ideal fuel source for long hikes and multiday backpacking trips. Because hiking demands steady energy output, incorporating fat-rich foods throughout the day can help you maintain a consistent energy base and reduces the need for constant carb refueling. Ultimately the goal is to have fats and carbs working together in your nutrition strategy to keep you moving strong from the trailhead to the summit and back again.

Beyond the trail and in the gym, healthy fats play a key role in recovery by helping to reduce inflammation and support muscle repair after a hard workout or hike. They also support hormone production—particularly testosterone—which is critical for building strength and improving your performance. Whether you're hiking long distances or training hard, balancing your intake of protein, carbs, and fats is the ultimate recipe for success.

Key Takeaways About Fats

Fats = Long-Lasting Energy: Unlike carbs, which burn quickly, fats provide steady, sustained energy for long endurance activities like hiking.

Support Recovery and Joint Health: Proper fat intake helps reduce inflammation, protects joints, and speeds up muscle recovery.

Eat the Right Fats: Prioritize whole food sources like nuts, seeds, avocados, eggs, and fatty fish, while avoiding processed seed oils and fried foods when possible.

Balance Is Key: Fats are nine calories per gram compared to four calories per gram like protein and carbs. Aim for **0.3 to 0.5 grams of fat per pound of bodyweight** to optimize performance and recovery without overeating calories. A high animal protein diet will usually check off the fat box too.

Nutrition Cheat Sheet

Protein	Carbohydrates	Fats
For muscle building, preservation, performance, and recovery postworkout or after a hike	Your primary energy source before, during, and after high-intensity workouts	For general bodily health and sustained energy during low-intensity physical activity
Animal meats Fish Eggs Beans	SIMPLE = Energy Now Sugary snacks Energy gels COMPLEX = Daily Energy Fruit Whole grains Potatoes	Egg yolks Avocados Nuts Seeds Fatty fish Coconut oil Olive oil

Now that we've covered the basics of protein, carbs, and fats—and now that you know more about nutrition than 95 percent of the population—let's bring it all together. It's time to create a nutritional strategy to support your training in the gym so your body can perform its best when you get on the trail. Strength gains and long miles await!

Nutrition Strategy for Your Training

When to Eat
- Preworkout meals: protein + carbs for energy 1 to 3 hours before training
- Postworkout meals: protein + carbs for recovery 0 to 2 hours after training

Remember earlier when I said you don't have to sweat the small stuff when it comes to timing your food? If you want the most optimal approach for your performance this will help you achieve that. At the end of the day as long as you eat the right amount of protein, carbs, fats, and calories you'll see great results.

James's Meal Prep Hack

Like anything in life, we can't improve what we don't measure. Whether it's the amount of calories you're eating or how much protein you're actually consuming, the more you track your food the better your results will be. With that said, however, finding a sustainable balance regarding the food you're eating and the energy spent tracking that food is important. Over the years my simple meal prep and macro hack involving just my plate has worked wonders for my clients and myself. It also requires zero thinking. Remember how I said I like to keep things simple?

Here's how I fill my plate to get the protein I need, the carbs I need (or don't need), and some fruits and vegetables with minimal effort.

1. Fill half the plate with meat/protein. Yes. Half.
2. Take the other half of the plate and fill one-third with carbs (rice, potatoes, pasta, fruit) and two-thirds with vegetables.

Depending on your goals and how hard you're training you may adjust your carbs to align with your goal and energy needs, but this is a great jumping off point to keep things simple and sustainable. Whether you need to consume more/fewer carbs, just portion that second half of your plate accordingly. The protein always remains the same though. Simple, effective, impactful. Give it a try.

Sample Nutrition Plan

Here is a sample day taken from one of my athletes' nutrition plans to give you an idea of what a day of eating for performance could look like.

For context she is forty years old, five feet five inches tall, 170 pounds, training for trail performance, and trying to cut down to 150 pounds. Her goal is to build strength and endurance for hiking while losing 20 pounds of body fat (aka the weight of her loaded hiking pack).

"I'm eating more food than I've ever eaten in a day, yet I'm losing weight and getting stronger every week. This is crazy!" —Julia A.

Daily Macro Totals

- Protein: ~155g
  - Breakfast: 30g
  - Morning Snack: 25g
  - Lunch: 45g
  - Afternoon Snack: 20g
  - Dinner: 35g
- Carbs: ~120g
- Calories: ~1,600

Breakfast
- Protein: 3 large eggs + 2 breakfast chicken sausages (30g protein, 300 calories)
- Side: 4 oz sweet potato (26g carbs, 100 calories)
- Veggie: 1 cup spinach (3g carbs, 20 calories)
- Total: 30g protein, 29g carbs, ~420 calories

Morning Snack
- Protein: 1 scoop protein shake (25g protein, 120 calories)
- Total: 25g protein, ~120 calories

Lunch
- Protein: 5 oz cooked chicken breast (45g protein, 220 calories)
- Side: 1/3 cup white rice (23g carbs, 110 calories)
- Veggie: 1 cup broccoli (6g carbs, 50 calories)
- Total: 45g protein, 29g carbs, ~380 calories

Afternoon Snack
- Protein: 1 cup nonfat Greek yogurt (20g protein, 100 calories)
- Carbs: 1/3 cup mixed berries (10g carbs, 50 calories) + 1 tbsp maple syrup (13g carbs, 50 calories)
- Total: 20g protein, 23g carbs, ~200 calories

Dinner
- Protein: 5 oz cooked sirloin steak (35g protein, 340 calories)
- Side: 4 oz roasted sweet potato (26g carbs, 100 calories)
- Veggie: 1 cup asparagus (5g carbs, 40 calories)
- Total: 35g protein, 31g carbs, ~480 calories

Consistency over Perfection

Just like with your training, when it comes to nutrition long-term consistency matters more than short-term perfection. Having a "cheat" meal (I hate that phrase) here and there is not going to matter when you take the long-term approach and keep showing up for yourself week after week.

The Refuel: Nutrition, Hydration, And Recovery

Nutrition is undoubtedly the "hardest" part of the equation for most people, but when you fall in love with the process of getting to your goals you build better habits and set yourself up for long-term success. You will also begin to notice that something amazing happens: The process eventually *becomes* the goal. That's when you've reached a new level in your training, nutrition, and mindset. Focus on consistency over perfection. Just like when you're on the trail, if you only focus on the summit you'll miss the trail, but when you fall in love with the trail (aka the process) you will always make it to the summit (aka the goal). More on this concept later in the book.

Your Nutrition Must Support Your Goals

There's a common saying within the fitness world: *"You can't out-train a bad diet."* While there may be some lucky genetic freaks out there who are simply gifted in this category, for the other 99 percent of us regular mortals, it's the honest truth. You're putting a lot of effort in the gym so you owe it to yourself to reap the rewards of that effort, and your nutrition is a giant piece of those results. Eat for your goals, train for performance, and everything else will usually fall into place when you're consistent.

Enjoying a summit and a sandwich while guiding an adventure on Iroquois Peak in the Adirondacks.

So before your next training session, ask yourself:

- **Did I eat enough protein and carbs today?**
- **Am I eating the right amount of calories for my goals?**
- **Am I following my nutrition plan properly?**

The stronger, more conditioned, and better prepared mountain athlete is the one who doesn't just train with intention but fuels with intention too. I have no doubt that you will be that mountain athlete.

Lift heavy and eat smart so you can hike hard. Your body will thank you.

Now that you have a strong foundation on nutrition, let's dive into the other important piece of the performance (and health) equation: hydration. So grab your hose and bladder and fill it up because we're about to talk all about water.

Hydration
Hydrate, Hydrate, Hydrate

Every time my body stopped working on the trail it was because I failed to hydrate. It's happened to me in the summer heat and in the dead of winter. Whether it was extreme fatigue, muscle cramps, or legs that locked up with each step, it was always because I got lazy with my hydration. These scenarios were my own fault and were entirely avoidable because they were in my control. I failed to control the controllables (more on that concept later). The mountains have enough factors outside our control, but your fitness, nutrition, and hydration are within your control. More life lessons courtesy of the mountains.

By now you know how to train hard and prepare your body to hike long miles. You know how to dial in your nutrition and make sure your protein, carbs, and fats are fueling your efforts efficiently. But there's one key element that often gets overlooked: hydration. And it's another important part of the performance equation.

Drink up. Enjoying a winter sunrise on Mt. Marcy, the tallest point in New York State.

Water is more than just something you casually sip throughout the day. It's the foundation of your body's ability to function at its highest level, which it can't do if you're dehydrated. Like when I bonked on McKenzie Mountain, dehydration shows up in the form of fatigue, cramps, dizziness, and, in some extreme cases, serious health risks in the backcountry.

Most people only think about water when they're thirsty, but waiting until you feel thirsty is like waiting until your gas tank is empty before filling up. Talk about a suboptimal approach, right? If dehydration sets in it's hard to recover from it, so it's best to be proactive and avoid it altogether. Whether you're grinding through a tough training session or backpacking through the mountains, your water intake is crucial for success. Now grab your highlighter and highlight this next sentence so you remember:

Hydration should be proactive, not reactive.

And it's not just about drinking enough water. Your body also needs electrolytes (sodium, potassium, magnesium, and calcium) to balance your hydration, keep your muscles working properly, and prevent that dreaded cramping. More on that shortly.

In this section, I'm going to give you a hydration strategy that supports your effort in the gym and on the trail so you stay ahead of hydration issues before they derail you. You'll learn why hydration is critical, how much water you actually need, when electrolytes factor in, and what to do if you start feeling dehydrated.

The bottom line is that if you want to lift stronger and recover faster so you can hike harder, your hydration strategy needs to be just as dialed in as your trail route and training. Let's talk about water.

Why Hydration Is Critical for Performance

Just like your high school biology teacher taught you, your body is roughly 60 percent water and every major function relies on it. So it's pretty important to say the least.

Proper hydration will

- **improve your strength and endurance.** Your muscles need water to contract efficiently. They can't work efficiently if you're dehydrated.
- **regulate your body temperature.** Sweat is like your body's cooling system, but if you don't replace the fluids lost you risk overheating.

- **prevent cramps and muscle fatigue.** When you sweat, you lose electrolytes (aka minerals) that help your muscles work properly. This imbalance is what leads to cramps, weakness, and fatigue. No one wants that when you're miles deep in the backcountry.
- **support recovery.** Water flushes waste products from your muscles after training or a long hike. So if you want to recover faster and reduce soreness, water and electrolytes need to be part of your pre-, intra-, and posttraining plan. This is nonnegotiable.

Now that you know why hydration matters, let's talk about how much water you actually need.

How Much Water Do You *Really* Need?

A common recommendation is to drink **half your bodyweight in ounces of water daily**. This is just your baseline though. When you're training hard or on the trail your water needs increase due to the increased exertion and water loss from sweat. So don't be shy, drink up!

Nalgene Bottle Strategy

Bodyweight: **250 pounds**
    Daily Hydration Requirement: **125+ fluid oz** (roughly 1 gallon)
        = **4** standard Nalgene (32 oz) bottles per day
Bodyweight: **200 pounds**
    Daily Hydration Requirement: **100+ fluid oz**
        = **3** standard Nalgene (32 oz) bottles per day
Bodyweight: **150 pounds**
    Daily Hydration Requirement: **75+ fluid oz**
        = **2.5** standard Nalgene (32 oz) bottles per day

Now that you understand the importance of water and how much to drink a day, is this a good time to tell you that water alone isn't always enough? We all know we sweat when we're working hard. If we're sweating it means we're losing electrolytes. Therefore we need to replenish those too so your body can actually absorb the water you're drinking. Let's talk about electrolytes.

What Are Electrolytes?

Have you ever been dehydrated on a hike, chugged a ton of water at the next river, and still felt sluggish, weak, and still cramping up? That's because there's more to the hydration equation than just drinking water. Welcome to the party, electrolytes.

Electrolytes help with

- **muscle function.** They help muscles contract and relax properly.
- **nerve signals.** Your brain and body communicate through signals powered by electrolytes.
- **hydration.** They help balance how much water is in your cells.
- **preventing cramps.** If you lose too many electrolytes, your muscles might cramp up.

In short, electrolytes keep your body running, help you avoid dehydration, and ensure your body actually absorbs the water you're drinking.

The Role of Each Electrolyte

Our bodies technically have seven essential electrolytes, but for our purposes these are the four we're focusing on and their roles.

- **Sodium:** Helps you retain water, maintain blood pressure, and prevent dizziness or brain fog. So toss some salt packets in your hiking pack just in case.
- **Potassium:** Regulates muscle contractions and prevents cramping. Grab a banana or other fruit.
- **Magnesium:** Helps with energy production and supports muscle relaxation to avoid tightness or spasms. Salted nuts or avocados work well here.
- **Calcium:** Plays a key role in nerve signaling and general muscle function. Think dairy products.

How You Lose Electrolytes

You lose electrolytes when you sweat, pee, or have diarrhea or vomiting. The more you sweat, the more you're losing. Remember when your mother kept telling you to *"drink your fluids"* every time you were home sick from school? Turns out she was onto something there. Moms truly do know best.

How to Replenish Electrolytes the Right Way

- **When Training or Hiking:** Put electrolyte tablets or powders in your water, or eat salty snacks (like salted nuts, jerky, salty potato chips).
- **Postworkout or Posthike:** Rehydrate with water and electrolytes.
- **Daily Maintenance:** Eat electrolyte-rich foods like bananas (potassium), nuts/seeds (magnesium), dairy (calcium), and salt your meals to taste (sodium).

How to Avoid Dehydration Before It Becomes a Problem

The best way to prevent dehydration is to stay ahead of it by consistently taking sips of water and replenishing salts before you feel like you need to. Remember the sentence you highlighted earlier about making hydration proactive, not reactive. Fend it off well before it has a chance of becoming an issue, especially on the trail. Now let's talk about the signs of dehydration and how to fix it.

Signs of Dehydration and How to Fix It

Sign of Dehydration	How to Fix It
Dry mouth, dizziness, headache	Drink 16 to 20 oz of water immediately
Muscle cramps, fatigue	Consume electrolytes (tablet, powder, banana, or salty snack)
Dark urine, low sweat production	Increase water intake, add sodium (salt)
Brain fog, irritability	Hydrate with water and electrolytes, eat a balanced meal

A good, practical hydration checkpoint is monitoring your urine:

- Light yellow = well hydrated.
- Dark yellow or orange = dehydration creeping in. Drink up. Salt up.

Trail and Training Hydration Strategy

Now that you understand the importance of hydration, here's a **simple game plan** to fend off dehydration in the gym and on the trail.

For the Gym:

1. **Preworkout:** 16 to 20 oz of water + electrolytes if training fasted.
2. **During Training:** Sip water throughout your workout. If you're sweating a lot, sip on an electrolyte drink. Bonus for adding a carbohydrate powder to your intraworkout water. Your energy and recovery time between sets will improve.
3. **Postworkout:** 20 to 30 oz of water + electrolytes + a meal with sodium/potassium.

For Hiking and Backpacking:

1. Before You Hike:
   - Drink 16 to 24 oz of water before heading out.
   - Eat a salty meal to boost your sodium levels.
   - Pack at least 1 liter per 2 hours of expected hiking time (more for hot weather).
2. During the Hike:
   - Drink half a liter (16 oz) per hour of movement.
   - Increase intake if it's hot, humid, or high altitude.
   - Use electrolyte tablets every 1 to 2 hours.
   - A 50/50 ratio of plain water-to-electrolyte-water is a good start.
   - Drink before you feel thirsty. Set a timer if you forget to drink.
3. Posthike Recovery:
   - Replace lost fluids with at least 1 liter of water.
   - Eat a sodium + potassium-rich meal (meat, potatoes, broth-based soups, etc.). Salt your meal to taste . . . seriously. Salt it.
   - Continue hydrating for the rest of the day.

Dehydration in the Winter? Yes. It Still Happens.

A reminder to all my fellow winter hikers out there, just because it's cold, hard to drink, and you're not "sweating" doesn't mean you need less water. You need to keep drinking. More of my dehydration woes have come in

January and February than in July or August. Be proactive and force yourself to stay hydrated.

Because we're talking about water and hiking, let's quickly touch on filtration in the backcountry so you have a battle-ready hydration strategy when you hit the trail.

Water in the Backcountry

When you're hiking I always recommend bringing *more* water than you expect to need, along with a water filtration system, and to locate all of your water sources on the map each day. Redundancy matters with hydration, and it's better to have too much water than not enough. With that in mind, I'm well aware carrying all your water isn't always practical or even possible. That's where a water filtration system comes in.

Some options include:

- **Water filters:** These are a good long-term, reliable purification option.
- **UV purifiers:** These kill bacteria and viruses in seconds.
- **Chemical drops/tablets:** Good lightweight option for emergency purification.

Your water sources for the day, and specifically your final water sources, are some of the most important things to locate on your map. Remember what I said earlier in the book about controlling what you can control on the trail? You can't control where the water sources are in the backcountry, but you can control your knowledge about where they are and when you'll pass them. Plan accordingly.

Proper Hydration Is a Nonnegotiable

Hydration isn't something you want to leave to chance. If you want to perform better, recover faster, and avoid miserable dehydration on the trail, your water and electrolyte strategy needs to be a priority. I have no doubts you will have this subject dialed in the next time you hit the trail or the gym.

So before your next training session or hike, ask yourself:

- **Did I drink enough water today?**
- **Have I replenished my electrolytes?**
- **Am I following my hydration plan?**

The Refuel: Nutrition, Hydration, And Recovery

A well-earned winter summit on Phelps Mountain with my Great Range Athlete PHELPS team.

The better-prepared mountain athlete is the one who doesn't just train hard but fuels and hydrates hard too. I have no doubt that you will be that mountain athlete.

So once again train hard, lift heavy, eat for your goals, and hydrate smart so you can hike strong. Your adventures will thank you.

Now it's time to build a nutritional game plan specifically for the trail so you're ready to perform your best in the backcountry. So fill up your Nalgene bottle, toss an electrolyte tablet in it, and keep reading.

ON-TRAIL NUTRITION STRATEGY

So you've done the sweaty, heart-pounding work to get your body strong prepared for the trail. You've eaten for performance so your strength and conditioning level is better than ever. Now it's time to hit the trail with a nutrition strategy that fuels your body from trailhead to trailhead with great success.

But first let me paint you a picture . . .

Imagine signing in at the trailhead full of energy as the sun shines through the evergreens, the birds chirping, with a gentle breeze blowing through the trees. You begin hiking and with every step you feel stronger, more confident, and more capable than the last. You approach your first major climb of the day and you scale it with ease, surprising yourself with how well you handled the elevation, leaving you wondering when it's going to start feeling "hard." Your legs keep climbing and before you know it you arrive at the summit where those hard-earned views await. Then you continue hiking and every step feels stronger than the last. Eventually you finish the trail without ever hitting a wall of exhaustion and confident you have more miles left in the tank.

Now imagine the opposite: dragging your feet, feeling sluggish, lightheaded, and cramping up throughout the climb, only to eventually stumble onto the summit running on fumes and feeling like you've been hit by a truck. The major differences between these two experiences come down to physical preparation. Training is one part of that equation, and nutrition strategy is the other.

Whether you're heading out for a day hike or a backpacking trip, your body needs fuel to keep moving efficiently. The right foods and fluids help you maintain energy, avoid muscle fatigue, and recover faster so you can enjoy every step of the adventure instead of suffering through it. Hiking's hard enough without the suffering.

This chapter is all about avoiding common mistakes and fueling yourself the right way so you can perform your best on the trail. We're going to take what you've learned about nutrition and apply it to give you a clear, actionable strategy for eating and drinking on the trail to stay hike strong mile after mile.

Common Trail Nutrition Mistakes

Whether I'm guiding clients in the Adirondack Mountains or hearing trail fail stories I see hikers make, these simple but costly mistakes often with their on-trail nutrition:

- **Undereating:** Simply not eating enough or just relying on a quick snack.
- **Relying on sugar alone:** Eating only high-sugar foods that often cause an energy crash.
- **Poor hydration strategy:** Drinking minimal water and never replacing electrolytes, leading to dehydration or worse.

The Four-Part Trail Nutrition Strategy That Works

Fueling for a hike isn't about random snacks in your pack; rather it's about strategically giving your body the right balance of food and hydration to perform its best. Each macronutrient (carbs, protein, fats) plays a specific role, and understanding how and when to use them properly can mean the difference between a strong, steady hike and one where you hit a wall. Remember, you're voluntarily putting yourself in difficult environments in the backcountry, so it's important to set yourself up for success whenever possible by controlling what you can control.

Let's go over my four-part strategy for trail nutrition success.

Part 1: Carbs: Your Primary Energy Source

Carbohydrates are your body's quickest and most efficient energy source. Your muscles burn carbs first, so you need to keep replenishing them throughout your hike. Load up to begin the day and eat throughout the day as your energy dictates.

Popular Trail Carbs:
- **Simple Carbs: Fast acting (aka quick energy now):** Honey, energy chews and gels, sugary snacks *(. . . if you must)*.
- **Complex Carbs: Slow digesting (aka longer-lasting energy):** Whole grain wraps, bread, bagels, oats, fruit, quinoa, rice.

When to Eat Carbs:
- **Before the hike:** A mix of slow and fast carbs (oatmeal with banana is great).
- **During the hike:** A small carb source every sixty to ninety minutes to keep energy levels up.
- **After the hike:** Carbs help replenish energy stores for recovery purposes.

Part 2: Protein: Essential for Recovery and Endurance

Protein isn't a quick energy source, but it prevents muscle breakdown and helps with endurance on long-distance hikes. It keeps you feeling full longer, which will help you hike harder. It's hard to perform well when your stomach is growling louder than the bear behind you, you know?

Popular Trail Proteins:
- Jerky
- Meat sticks
- Deli meat
- Protein bars
- Tuna or chicken packets
- Nut butter packets

When to Eat Protein:
- **Before the hike:** A high-protein meal to prepare your body for the day (eggs, meat, and whole grain toast).
- **During the hike:** If hiking all day, include protein in a meal (jerky, bagged chicken or tuna, meat stick, or meat on a sandwich).
- **After the hike:** Eat a balanced high-protein meal with complex carbs.

Part 3: Fats: Long-Lasting Fuel for the Trail

Fats keep you energized throughout your day. They take longer to break down, making them a slow, steady energy source—perfect for long hikes. They're not great for quick energy bursts though—your carbs provide that. Just remember that carbs are for energy *now*, and fats are for energy *later*.

Popular Trail Fats:
- Nuts (almonds, cashews, walnuts)
- Seeds (pumpkin, sunflower, chia)
- Cheese
- Dark chocolate
- Avocado

When to Eat Fats:
- **Before the hike:** A moderate amount (peanut butter on whole grain toast).
- **During the hike:** Best in small amounts to avoid sluggishness (trail mix with nuts and chocolate).
- **After the hike:** Helps with recovery and staying full (rice, potatoes, avocado).

Part 4: Hydration and Electrolytes

You learned in the last chapter that water alone isn't enough and that you need electrolytes (sodium, potassium, magnesium, calcium) to prevent dehydration, muscle cramps, and fatigue.

How to Stay Hydrated:
- **Before the hike:** Drink 20 oz of water with electrolytes.
- **During the hike:** Sip water consistently (0.5 liter per hour) and add electrolytes if sweating heavily. I like a 50/50 split of drinking plain water and electrolyte water.
- **After the hike:** Rehydrate with another 20 oz of water with electrolytes.

Popular Electrolyte Sources:
- Electrolyte tablets or powders
- Sports drinks (low sugar)
- Salted nuts or pretzels
- Pickles or pickle juice (yes . . . seriously)

On-Trail Nutrition Cheat Sheet
- **Carbs = Fast energy now** (eat regularly).
- **Protein = Muscle endurance** (eat strategically).
- **Fats = Long-lasting energy later** (eat in moderation).
- **Electrolytes = Hydration balance** (water *and* electrolytes).

Now you know what food to eat, when to eat it, and why you're eating it so you have a full-fledged nutrition plan the next time you hit the trail. Whether you're out for a day hike, a simple overnight, or long-distance backpacking, the same principles apply. The implementation may change but the principles of what food your body needs and when it needs them will not. I have no doubts you will notice a major uptick in how good you feel on the trail when you execute this strategy.

Protein and Long-Distance Backpacking

Let's talk about long-distance backpacking. There's a common misconception among the backpacking community that carrying and consuming a high-protein diet on the trail isn't feasible. I disagree. Like everything else, it requires intentionality and choices. Due to my controversial hot take, I reached out to my good friend Paul Fuzinski from Aptitude Outdoors to get his opinion on this. Paul is an expert outdoorsman, avid Crossfitter, and long-distance backpacker (Appalachian Trail Class of 2015). Like all of you reading this book, Paul values his hard-earned muscle and strength built in the gym as much as he values backcountry adventure.

Here's what Paul had to say about the protein and long-distance backpacking debate:

Hiking blogs and forums are filled with food ideas for backpacking with everything from expensive freeze-dried meals to candy bars and beer. I've tried them all while thru-hiking the Appalachian Trail and on other long-distance adventures. At the end of the day, eat what you want—but if you want to maintain your hard-earned muscle, protein is key.

There's a common myth that protein is heavy and hard to pack. Not true. You can find high-protein options even at gas stations or dollar stores. Peanut butter, for example, packs 8g+ of protein per serving and is one of the best calorie-dense trail foods out there. It's not necessarily what I'd consider a protein source at home, but when you're backpacking it's a great choice all things considered.

Trail mix has long been a backpacking staple, offering a great balance of protein, fats, and carbs. And then there's jerky, the king of trail protein, with 30g+ per bag. It's lightweight and it's available everywhere. A great choice for backpackers.

Cured meats like salami or pepperoni are surprisingly shelf-stable and great for quick protein hits—just don't overdo it unless you want an upset stomach. Tuna and chicken foil packs are probably the best bang for your buck protein bombs (16–22g), lightweight, and full of sodium to help with hydration. And for you brave souls, even SPAM or sardines can pack 13–24g of protein per serving and can be easily carried. Everything tastes good after a long day of hiking.

Protein bars (20–30g) are easy to stash and don't spoil. Protein powder is another efficient option since you just mix it in with coffee or water. And don't sleep on powdered milk either because it's decent protein at around 10g and also adds creaminess to any hot meal.

Additionally every time you pass through a town you can make sure you eat a large amount of protein before going back into the woods. That

The Refuel: Nutrition, Hydration, And Recovery

should definitely be part of your strategy. You can easily get 50–100g of protein in a single meal in town. It all helps.

The bottom line is that you've got plenty of options. With a little creativity and planning, you absolutely can maintain a high-protein diet on the trail no matter what some internet gram weenies tell you. Plus, then you won't lose all your upper body muscle on your backpacking trip. Have fun!
—*Paul Fuzinski*
Aptitude Outdoors
Appalachian Trail Class of 2015

High-Protein Trail Shopping List

When you're backpacking it's critical to recover, maintain lean muscle, and keep your metabolism firing. But getting 175 to 200g of protein a day while living out of a backpack? That takes planning, but it can be done.

Below is a trail-tested shopping list of protein-packed, shelf-stable foods you can grab from most grocery stores or order ahead of time. No fridge required. This is meant to give you some ideas for your next backpacking trip.

Backpackers Protein Shopping List

Proteins:
- **Jerky:** 10g per ounce
- **Tuna or chicken packets:** 20 to 25g per pouch (look for foil pouches, not cans)
- **Dehydrated meat or freeze-dried meals**: 40 to 60g per meal
- **Protein powder:** 20 to 30g per scoop
- **Shelf-stable tofu or tempeh:** 10 to 15g per serving (limited use item due to weight)
- **Powdered peanut butter:** 8g per 2 tbsp
- **Hard cheese (like aged parmesan or wax-wrapped cheddar):** 7 to 10g per ounce
- **Powdered eggs:** 6g per serving
- **Dry roasted edamame:** 13g per 1/4 cup
- **Lentil or chickpea pasta (precooked or rehydrated):** 13g+ per serving
- **Textured vegetable protein (TVP):** 12g per 1/4 cup (just add water)

Protein Snacks:
- **Protein bars:** 15 to 20g
- **Trail mix with jerky and nuts:** 10g per handful
- **Roasted chickpeas:** 6g per 1/4 cup
- **Nut butter packets (almond, peanut):** 7g per packet
- **Granola and protein powder mix:** 20g+
- **Shelf-stable protein shakes:** 20 to 40g (for shorter trips)

A High-Protein Backpacking Meal Plan (180g+ Protein)

This day assumes you're hiking long distances and carrying a moderate to heavy pack.
Total calories = 3,000 to 3,500 depending on fat/carb choices.

Breakfast (45g Protein):
- Instant oats + 1 scoop protein powder (30g)
- 1 tbsp powdered peanut butter (4g)
- Instant coffee + powdered creamer
- Trail mix handful with jerky bits (10g)

Mid-Morning Snack (20g):
- 1 protein bar (20g)

Lunch (38g):
- Tuna packet (20g) on 2 tortillas
- Nut butter packet (7g)
- Trail mix handful (10g)

Afternoon Snack (20g):
- Roasted edamame or chickpeas (13g)
- Small protein shake or another bar (7 to 10g)

Dinner (60g):
- Freeze-dried high-protein meal (40 to 60g depending on brand)
- Optional: Add extra protein powder or drink a shake

Evening Snack (Optional, 10g):
- Peanut butter tortilla wrap
- Small scoop protein powder in water or cocoa packet

I'm confident that a high-protein diet on the trail will make you feel the difference. Your strength lasts longer, soreness fades faster, and you'll recover better when protein is dialed in. An effective nutrition strategy has protein, carbs, and fats working together, so don't neglect your protein when you're backpacking. Your body needs it to perform at its best and recover each night.

Fail to Plan = Plan to Fail

Having a nutrition (aka fuel) strategy in place the next time you go hiking will have an immediate impact on your performance, leading to stronger, more fulfilling adventures.

Before your next hike go through your food and ask yourself:

- **Do I have protein for substance, performance, and recovery?**
- **Do I have "fast" carbs for energy NOW?**
- **Do I have fats for energy LATER?**
- **Do I have enough water and electrolytes for the hike?**

Everyone prepares their backpacks and gear. That's the easy part. Few people prepare their fitness and nutrition strategy for the trail with the same focus. You are now among the few. I commend you for rising above the status quo.

Now that we've covered how to train to build those trail muscles, and how to eat and hydrate for performance on and off the trail, let's discuss the most overlooked piece of the equation when it comes to physical fitness: recovery.

RECOVERY: THE MOST OVERLOOKED FACTOR IN TRAIL READINESS
Recover, Recover, Recover

Muscle and strength are *not* built in the gym and they're certainly not built on the trail. Yes you read that correctly. What you're actually doing in the gym and on the trail is *breaking down* those muscles. They're built during the recovery process. This is why recovery is so important for any athletic pursuit. Earlier in the book I mentioned how it's easy for most hikers to obsess over gear and neglect training; it's also easy to obsess over training and neglect recovery from that training.

Unfortunately I see this time and time again from hikers and athletes alike. By ignoring recovery you're

1. breaking down your muscles but not optimally rebuilding them leading to poor results for your efforts . . . and a higher risk for injury and

A chilly, colorful winter sunrise on Cascade Mountain.

2. slowing down or even stalling your progress altogether because you're unable to push hard when you train or hike. This ultimately leads to feeling burned out before you even hit the trail.

Trap bar deadlifts.

Feeling burned out before you hike probably isn't ideal considering the goal is to become your best on the trail, you know?

Training is the stressor and recovery is the repair process where you come back stronger, faster, and more prepared than before.

In this chapter, you're going to learn exactly how to recover like an athlete so you can train harder, hike stronger, and feel better without burning out.

The Three Parts of Recovery: Sleep, Nutrition, and Movement

People often equate recovery as an excuse to do nothing in the name of "rest days." I challenge you to be better than that. Recovery isn't about doing nothing; it's about doing more with intention to give your body what it needs to rebuild and come back stronger.

There are three major parts of recovery: **sleep, nutrition, and movement.** When you get these dialed in you'll get better results and feel stronger than ever.

Part 1: Sleep

If there's one nonnegotiable when it comes to recovery, it's sleep. You can have the best training plan in the world and a clean diet, but if you're skimping on sleep, you're robbing yourself of the results you're working hard to obtain.

Why Sleep Matters

- **Muscle Growth and Repair:** Sleep is when your muscles rebuild from training. If you cut sleep short you're likely cutting your progress short too.
- **Hormone Optimization:** Testosterone, human growth hormone (HGH), and cortisol (aka the stress hormone) are all regulated by sleep. So a lack of sleep leads to increased stress and poor muscle recovery.
- **Cognitive and Decision-Making Skills:** In the backcountry, making the wrong decision can be dangerous. A tired mind leads to mistakes—whether it's misjudging terrain, missing a trail marker, or pushing too hard and ignoring warning signs from your body. Our minds need to be clear and sharp out there.

- **Energy and Endurance:** Poor sleep equals poor energy levels. And when you're climbing a mountain or lifting a weight, every ounce of energy matters.

How to Improve Sleep for Maximum Recovery

- Aim for seven to nine hours of sleep per night. Your body does its best work in deep sleep.
- Create a nighttime routine: Dim the lights, avoid screens, and wind down before bed.
- Keep your room cool and dark for optimal sleep quality.
- If you struggle with sleep, cut caffeine after 2 p.m.

Treat sleep like a mandatory part of your training. If you're serious about building strength and endurance, you need to be serious about sleep. Plus, who doesn't love long nights of sleep and waking up refreshed? I certainly do.

Part 2: Nutrition and Hydration

Your body can't recover if it doesn't have the right fuel. Proper nutrition and hydration are just as important as your training itself. So if you're undereating, skipping protein, or not drinking enough water, you're self-sabotaging your own efforts to get stronger, recover faster, and go farther. Let's ensure that doesn't happen with a nutrition recap because it deserves to be learned.

The Four Essentials of Recovery Nutrition

Protein for Muscle

- Strength training breaks down muscle, but protein rebuilds it stronger.
- Aim for one gram of protein per pound of ideal bodyweight.
- The best protein sources include meat, eggs, fish, Greek yogurt, cottage cheese, and protein shakes.

Carbs for Energy

- Carbs replenish energy stores in your muscles after training or hiking.
- After a workout or long hike, eat plenty of carbs to refuel.

- The best carb sources include complex carbs that digest slowly and simple carbs that digest quickly.

Fats for Function and Energy

- Healthy fats reduce inflammation and support hormone production for muscle recovery.
- The best fat sources include avocados, nuts, olive oil, fatty fish, and eggs.

Water and Electrolytes for Hydration

- Aim for at least half your bodyweight in ounces of water daily.
- Add electrolytes to your water before, during, and after workouts and hikes
- The best electrolyte sources include adding sea salt or electrolyte tablets or powder to your water and eating whole foods rich in potassium and magnesium (bananas, avocados, nuts).

Along with proper sleep, getting your nutrition and hydration dialed in will set up your body for success. You'll get rid of that soreness faster. Speaking of soreness, let's discuss the most forgotten piece of the recovery phase: movement.

Part 3: Movement, aka "Active Recovery"

Most people think resting means doing nothing, but that's actually one of the worst things you can do for recovery. Your body is a lot stronger than you think it is. It wants to move. Your brain may want to lounge on the couch all day, but your body craves movement. In my experience the best way to recover faster, eliminate soreness, and feel ready for your next training session is to move.

This is called active recovery.

Why Movement Helps Recovery

- **Flushes out soreness (Delayed onset muscle soreness [DOMS]):** Blood flow helps reduce muscle stiffness and speeds up recovery. If muscles are sore, get blood flow to the area through movement.

- **Keeps joints healthy:** Moving through a full range of motion prevents tightness and stiffness from setting in. Sore quads? Do some bodyweight squats and watch them loosen up.
- **Prepares you for your next workout:** The quicker you recover, the harder you can train in your next session, and the better your results will be.

Best Active Recovery Techniques

- **Zone 2 Cardio:** Low-intensity hiking, walking, cycling, or swimming to promote blood flow without adding fatigue. This level of movement should feel good.
- **Mobility Work:** Hip, ankle, and thoracic spine mobility drills.
- **Foam Rolling and Massage:** Helps release muscle tension and break up tight areas.
- **Stretching:** Focus on hips, hamstrings, quads, calves, shoulders, and upper back to maintain flexibility and prevent stiffness.
- **Movement "Snacks":** If you're feeling stiff, take two to three minutes every hour to get up and move. My go-to favorites are bodyweight squats, jumping jacks, and shoulder circles.

Rower. A great, low-impact endurance builder.

Muscle Recovery Strategy

Postworkout Protocol:
- Rehydrate with electrolytes immediately following workout (16 to 20 oz).
- Eat a high-protein, high-carb meal zero to two hours following your workout when possible.
- Spend five to ten minutes foam rolling, doing mobility drills, and/or walking at a brisk pace.
- Sleep for seven to nine hours.

Trail Recovery Protocol

Before the Hike
- Eat a high-protein, high-carb meal one to two hours before hiking.

During the Hike
- Sip electrolyte water consistently
- Snack on protein, fats, and carbs to maintain steady energy.
- Take short, thirty-second stretching and mobility breaks every few hours to stay fresh and avoid tightness. A little goes a long way.

Posthike Recovery
- Rehydrate immediately with electrolytes.
- Eat a full meal with protein and carbs to refuel your muscles.
- Foam roll or stretch before bed to help minimize soreness.
- Get seven to nine hours of sleep.

Train Hard and Recover Hard So You Can Adventure Harder

If you want results in the gym you must train hard, but the smartest athletes focus on recovering hard too. Whether you're in the gym or on the trail, the more boxes you check for recovery the better you'll perform tomorrow.

Your Recovery Checklist:
- **Hydration:** Water + electrolytes.
- **Nutrition:** Protein, carbs, and healthy fats support muscle repair and endurance.

- **Sleep:** Seven to nine hours is a must for full recovery.
- **Movement:** Active recovery speeds up muscle repair and reduces soreness.

Prioritize the three parts of recovery: sleep, nutrition, and movement. Take a mental note of how you feel when you do versus when you do not. Once these items become a nonnegotiable in your training routine you'll be stronger, faster, and more resilient than ever for whatever the mountains throw at you.

The Next Step

At this point in your journey you know exactly how to train to get physically strong and conditioned for hiking, how to eat for success on and off the trail, and now you know how to recover so you can lift heavy and hike hard. Now it's time to continue up this mountain and discuss arguably the most important factor of backcountry success: your mindset.

I assure you that your brain will quit far sooner than your legs will. So let's get that strong too.

CHAPTER 5

The Trail Split: Mindset for the Mountains

IN HIKING, A *TRAIL SPLIT* IS THE MOMENT THE PATH DIVIDES AND YOU HAVE to choose which direction to go. It's a literal fork in the trail—and the choice is yours. In life, it's no different. Your actions determine your path forward, and your mindset is the compass guiding those actions.

"I'm turning around . . . this is too hard . . ." —James Appleton (2009)

As I mentioned at the beginning of this book, the climb up McKenzie Mountain was not the only time a trail got the better of me. On McKenzie, my body bonked, but on a different mountain a few years before that, it was my mind that let me down.

The year was 2009 and I was in my early twenties when my friends talked me into joining them on a hike in the Adirondack High Peaks. "Don't worry . . . it's one of the easier High Peaks," my buddy Jon said. Reluctantly I agreed to join them for a fall hike up Big Slide Mountain. I had hiked a few mountains with them in the past but it was always a major struggle. Why? Because I was overweight and lazy.

My friends picked me up early that morning and we drove to the trailhead and began hiking. Unlike most Adirondack High Peaks, Big Slide doesn't have a long approach, so the trail begins climbing right from the start. The first couple miles gained roughly 2,500 feet of elevation. Quickly, I fell behind.

Less than fifteen minutes after signing in at the trailhead, already covered in sweat and gasping for air from the immediate and seemingly "relentless" climb, I yelled up the trail, *"Hey guys. I need a break."* They stopped and we took a break so I could catch my breath and contemplate my life choices. Ten minutes later we put our packs back on and continued hiking. Like before, I fell behind again. I couldn't help but notice how heavy I was breathing compared to the others. Every so often they'd stop to let me catch up but then continue hiking only for me to fall behind again.

I told them I needed a break again. This time I was the only person who took off his backpack though. It was painfully obvious this hike was harder for me than it was for them. After refueling and catching my breath a second time we continued up the trail, but like clockwork the distance between us grew quickly. They moved further up the mountain and I became sweatier and sweatier, huffing and puffing more with every step.

Then the voices in my head started chirping, *"Dude, there's no way you can do this all day. Besides, no one's making you be here . . ."* Frustrated and defeated, I yelled out for a third time *"Hey guys . . . wait up"*. Once I caught up to the group I boldly declared, **"*I'm turning around . . . this is too hard . . .*"** Surprised and confused, they all tried talking me out of it. After all, we were probably only an hour into the hike, but I had already made up my mind. I was turning around. Oh, and I also decided that hiking sucks.

Embarrassed, I took Jon's car keys, said goodbye, and turned around. It was a long, lonely, disappointing walk back down the mountain to the car. A walk that involved a pit in my stomach of frustration and embarrassment with myself. I couldn't even climb an "easy" High Peak because I was so out of shape physically . . . and mentally.

To add insult to injury, later in the day I had to return to the trailhead to pick them back up, adding a log to the fire of my embarrassing failure. They were all smiles ear to ear after a great mountain adventure. I heard the trail stories I missed out on. The real gut punch, however, came when Jon told me,

> *"We were literally two minutes away from the first summit when you turned around. You should have kept going. It got a lot easier."*

A devastating blow and a life lesson to be learned. Not only did I miss out on the stories, the camaraderie, the victories, and the views that day, but **I chose to quit on myself when things got hard**. I chose giving up instead of persevering. I chose weakness instead of strength and resilience. Just minutes before the payoff of the first summit no less. All because of a little heavy breathing and sweat?

Beyond my obvious physical fitness woes the Adirondack High Peaks revealed something else that day: how mentally weak I was. They showcased how quickly I quit on myself all because of the story I kept playing in my head saying, *"This is too hard."* The mountains are good at revealing our weaknesses though.

The Trail Split: Mindset for the Mountains

The mountains will always remain unchanged whether we make it to the summit or not. It's our choice to either persevere or give up when things get hard. And that is a choice that we fully control. The Adirondack Mountains taught me a valuable life lesson that day.

Speaking of learning valuable life lessons in the mountains . . .

THE MOUNTAINS ARE THE ULTIMATE EQUALIZER
Nothing is guaranteed in the backcountry. The summit doesn't care that you took time off work to hike. The trail doesn't care how hard you trained. The weather certainly doesn't care about your plans.

There are no handouts out there and it's solely up to you to get yourself to the summit and back to the trailhead. No one else can hike for you. What I love about hiking is that the mountains don't care who you are, what trails you've hiked before, what fancy gear you bought, how much money you make, or how many followers you have on social media. The backcountry is the ultimate equalizer. It's up to you, your legs, your lungs, and your mind to keep moving forward. Everybody is given the same opportunity to succeed. The mountains truly are a direct reflection of real life, although I'd say the sights, sounds, and smells are a little nicer out there than they are in real life, but I digress.

That's exactly why the mountains are one of the purest teachers on the planet. They may not *care* about you, but they will *teach* you about life and yourself if you're willing to listen to them.

I believe the biggest determining factor in whether you succeed or fail in the backcountry is your mindset. Physical strength, endurance, and skill will get you far, but mental toughness is what gets you to the finish line when things get hard. Because at some point, the mountains and trails will test you. Oh, and spoilers—it's going to get hard.

Most people break the first moment their brain tells them, "*This is too hard.*" They look for an excuse to quit just like I did that day on Big Slide Mountain. But those who succeed? They're the ones who know how to embrace discomfort, how to positively control their mindset in negative conditions, and how to push forward even when every part of them is looking for that reason to quit. And these lessons aren't just about hiking either—they're about life.

The way you show up in the mountains is usually the way you show up everywhere else too. When things get hard in life, do you quit easily, or do you persevere? Do you let obstacles stop you, or do you find a way around them? Do you let fear dictate your actions, or do you take control and keep pushing forward? Do you let past failures define you, or do you learn from them and come back stronger every time?

Just like the backcountry, life will throw you curveballs, but that doesn't mean you can't still swing the bat and hit the ball over the center field fence.

Developing the ability to keep moving forward on the hardest, steepest, muddiest, wettest, bug-infested days isn't just a skill for the mountains—it's a skill for life. Challenges don't just exist on the trail; they show up in our daily struggles, our setbacks, and the moments that test us when no one is watching. And because we spend far more time within the four walls of our daily lives than we do in the backcountry, we owe it to the mountains to take the lessons they teach us and apply them beyond the trail. Because true growth as hikers and as people comes from experiencing those lessons and then choosing to live by them.

This chapter isn't just about building the necessary mental toughness and mindset for the mountains; it's also about carrying that same mindset into every aspect of your life. Because if you think hiking is only about hiking, then you're missing the bigger picture. There's a lot more juice to squeeze out of the trail than just some nice views, the sounds of flowing rivers, and the scent of pine. The mountains have the ability to make us all stronger versions of ourselves top to bottom, inside and out. This chapter is going to teach you to look for those lessons so you can awaken that version of yourself no matter where your feet take you.

BUILDING MENTAL TOUGHNESS FOR THE BACKCOUNTRY—AND YOUR LIFE

So what exactly is "mental toughness"?

I define mental toughness as **having the ability to stay focused, composed, and resilient in the face of challenges**. It's what keeps you moving forward toward your goal when everything inside you wants to give up.

In the mountains, it's what pushes you up the final climb when your feet hurt, the rain is pouring, the summit is out of sight, and self-doubt starts to creep in.

In the gym, it's what gets you to show up and train on the days you don't feel like it, it's inconvenient, or you're "too busy" (PSA: Your health and fitness goals don't care how "busy" you think your schedule is. Priorities.)

But again mental toughness isn't just for the backcountry. It's for your career, your relationships, your health, and every goal you're striving to achieve.

Because when life throws you into the storm, no one is coming to rescue you. Just like in the mountains, you have to adapt, persevere, push forward, and take complete ownership of your situation.

However, mental toughness is not about being "fearless." On the contrary. It's about acting *despite* the fear you feel. It's about standing in the face of adversity and choosing to keep going. It's about accepting that growth is only on the other side of "hard."

The good news is that just like physical strength and endurance, mental toughness is built. And the mountains are one of the best places to build it. In this section you're going to learn the four Cs of mental toughness, how to build it, and how to use your newfound resilience to your advantage everywhere.

Four Cs of Mental Toughness

To build an unshakable mindset that will serve you well on the trail and in your life, you need a solid foundation. These four Cs (commitment, control, challenge, and confidence) are that foundation. They can help you become the type of person who pushes through challenges instead of giving up when things get hard. Because overcoming "hard" things is the name of the game.

Let's begin with "commitment."

1. COMMITMENT: Standards over Emotions

What It Means

Commitment is the choice to stay dedicated to your goals no matter how hard it gets. It's about prioritizing the work required to accomplish your goal regardless of your motivation level. We all know motivation comes and goes, but commitment takes things to a new level where you operate on standards rather than emotions. Those who win in life don't let their emotions dictate their actions, their standards do.

On the Trail

When the summit or destination feels out of reach, commitment keeps you moving forward one step at a time. Moving forward one step at a time will guarantee you make it. It may not always be pretty or at the speed you want, but you *will* make it to the summit, and that's what matters.

In the Gym

There's always reasons (aka excuses) not to train: "busy" day at work, "short" on time, you "don't feel well," the list goes on. Commitment, however, is what gets you to show up even when you don't feel like it. That's what separates the people who achieve their fitness goals from the ones who never do. We may not always be able to give 100 percent every day, but showing up day after day, and giving everything we can give for that day, is the secret sauce to physical fitness. Adopting an "anything eats nothing" mentality is how you win. Commitment builds that mentality.

In Life

Commitment is what separates those who talk about their goals from those who actually put in the work to achieve them. It's the daily decision to keep showing up for yourself, even when you're feeling unmotivated or nobody's watching. Commitment builds integrity with yourself so you always do what you say you're going to do.

How to Strengthen COMMITMENT

1. **Define your WHY:** Know WHY you're doing something. What's your bigger, deeper purpose? Let that be your North Star.
2. **Visualize the outcome:** Picture yourself reaching the "summit" (that is, goal) and stay focused on that feeling of success. The mind is a powerful thing.
3. **Build accountability:** Share your goal with someone who will keep you honest. The more mechanisms for accountability you install in your life, the more likely you are to achieve your goals. It's easy to let ourselves down; it's a lot harder to let other people down. Use that to your advantage for success.

2. CONTROL: The Controllables, Prepare for the Uncontrollables

What It Means

Control is focusing on what you *can* control and preparing for what you *can't*. It's important to know the differences between planning and preparing. In short, plan what you can control and be prepared for what you can't. This will minimize frustration and maximize your ability to adapt when things outside your control don't go according to plan.

The Trail Split: Mindset for the Mountains

On the Trail

You can't control the weather, the terrain, the wildlife, or how steep the ascent is, but you *can* control your physical preparation, your knowledge of the terrain, your nutrition, your gear, and your attitude. There are so many things entirely outside our control in the backcountry, so it's our job to be prepared for those things and to control what we can. Control the controllables and control them well.

In the Gym

You can't always control your schedule or unexpected things that come up in life, but you can control the effort you give when you train. Some days you may have an hour; other days you may only have ten minutes. Effort is always in your control. You can control the food you eat to support the training you're doing. You can control the training program you're running and whether or not you see it through to the end. These are all within your control. Once again, control the controllables and control them well.

In Life

You can't control setbacks, difficult people, or unexpected challenges, but you *can* control your response. Do you harp on problems or do you focus on finding solutions? Do you let challenges break you or do you seek to overcome them? That's where your power truly lies. Never underestimate how monumental that power is.

How to Strengthen CONTROL

1. **Deep breaths:** "Take a deep breath and let's pause for a moment." You've heard it a million times for a reason. A deep breath resets your mind and shifts your focus to the controllables.
2. **Ask yourself, "What CAN I do right now?":** Direct your energy toward solutions, not problems. Focus on what you *can* do right now; don't harp on what you can't do.
3. **Prepare for the unexpected:** Expect obstacles to arise. That way when they do show up, you're already prepared to handle them.

3. CHALLENGE: Reframe Obstacles as Opportunities

What It Means

Seeing obstacles as opportunities for growth. This is easier said than done sometimes, but if we aim for this mindset we'll tackle challenges differently.

We only get stronger when we're stretched beyond our comfort zones. Just like muscles don't grow if you don't challenge them, we don't grow if we aren't challenged. So when obstacles arise tell yourself, "Game on!" and watch what you're capable of overcoming. Remember, growth is always uncomfortable, but it's always on the other side of hard.

On the Trail

The steepest, hardest climbs often lead to the best views, but you have to be willing to push through discomfort to earn those views. Then the next time you'll be stronger and more confident than the last. When you do this over and over again no summit will be out of reach. Hard days on the trail are major opportunities to show yourself what you're truly made of. Those days are where growth is generated and confidence is built.

In the Gym

Consistently challenging yourself in the gym is a cheat code for a strong mind and life. We only get stronger when we push ourselves outside our comfort zones. Muscles only grow when they need to lift more. So if you aren't challenging yourself by pushing beyond your current threshold, you're not going to get the results you want.

The gym is the best place to practice challenging yourself because it's a controlled environment. This way when the uncontrollables in life or on the trail arise, you've already built trust with yourself that you can do hard things. Training builds your mind as much as it builds your muscles.

In Life

Growth lives outside of your comfort zone. If you're always looking for the easy way, you're missing the chance to become something greater. Viewing obstacles as opportunities for growth will prepare your mind to overcome hard things in every aspect of life.

How to Strengthen CHALLENGE

1. **Reframe "hard":** Instead of thinking, "*This is too hard,*" shift your perspective to, "*This will make me stronger. Good. Keep going.*"
2. **Set incremental goals:** Push yourself a little harder and a little further each time—in the gym, on the trail, and in your life. Getting to a summit requires a lot of small steps. Achieving your goal is no different.

3. **Seek discomfort regularly:** The more comfortable you get being uncomfortable, the stronger you'll become. When something scares you, lean into it because growth comes from the struggle. Don't shy away from doing "hard" things; instead remind yourself that you're hard too. You got this.

4. CONFIDENCE: Building Self-Belief Through Preparation

What It Means

Confidence is *not* arrogance. It's that quiet, unwavering belief that you *are* capable. And that self-belief is built through your preparation.

On the Trail

Confidence is knowing that when you stand at the trailhead, you're prepared for the hike in every aspect. You've trained for the terrain, you've done your prehike homework, and you're fully prepared for the adventure because you controlled the controllables and prepared for the uncontrollables.

In the Gym

Few people will ever test themselves with a one-rep max on the squat. However, there are few feelings in the world like unracking the barbell for a new personal record (PR) attempt and immediately knowing *"Yes. I can lift this."* If you know, you know. It's a confidence builder like no other.

Setting PRs in the gym is an amazing feeling, and a feeling that should be chased forever. PRs only come from doing the work that leads to them. Every time you set a new PR you're building an unparalleled confidence in your ability to put in the hard work to get the outcome you desire. This will translate to your self-confidence on the trail and in your life. Guaranteed.

In Life

Confidence is knowing that you are capable of overcoming any challenge life throws your way. It doesn't mean the challenge won't be hard or the road won't be ugly, but it's a belief that you're prepared to handle that challenge no matter what.

How to Strengthen CONFIDENCE

1. **Celebrate every small win:** You can't move a mile without moving an inch first. Every step forward is a win and every win leads to the next. Wins build confidence. They're all important.

2. **Train with purpose:** Remind yourself that every rep, every hike, and every tough moment is preparing you for something bigger.
3. **Intentionally challenge yourself:** Challenge yourself on purpose even when no one is watching. The more "reps" you get, the more confident you'll become in your ability to overcome real challenges.
4. **Imagine your success:** See yourself coming out victorious on the "summit" and stay focused on that visual.

A Strong Body Builds a Strong Mind and a Strong Mind Builds a Strong Life

Every time you push through exhaustion to go one more mile, lift one more rep, navigate unexpected obstacles, or battle that self-doubt that creeps in on you like a silent deer in the woods, you're sharpening your mental toughness for *everything* life will throw at you.

Because let's be honest, most of life's hardest challenges don't happen on a trail. They happen in your daily life, in your relationships, in your career, and in the moments that test your character.

So I encourage you to take what the trail teaches you and apply it well.

When challenges arise, lean into them and control the controllables. When you feel like quitting, just go one more step . . . then another . . . then another. When life gets hard, remember these four Cs because they'll serve you well. Learn them. Implement them. Live by them.

And when it's time to climb your next mountain—whether literal or figurative—you'll be more prepared than ever because strength isn't just about muscles or weight on a bar, it's a mindset.

And the mountains give you the tools to build an unshakable one.

Five Life Lessons from the Trail

Most people think of hiking and backpacking as just a physical pursuit. They think of it as a way to enjoy some nice views and breathe the fresh air but fail to look beyond that. The backcountry offers much more than views and flowing rivers though; it's one of the greatest classrooms you'll ever step into.

While there are thousands of lessons to be learned from the trail—a subject that could warrant its own book alone—here are my five backcountry life lessons that will serve you well on your journey of life.

Lesson #1: The Best Things in Life Take Effort, and Effort Is Free

Nothing worthwhile comes easy. Not a summit. Not strength. Not success.

Everything in life that's worth having, whether it's fitness, confidence, resilience, or self-respect, is earned through effort. There are no shortcuts to get there and they can't be bought. The effort you put in is free, and every person has the same opportunity to give a 100 percent effort.

Both the trail and the barbell teach you this in a way that no motivational quote or self-help book ever could.

- You *earn* every mile hiked and mountain summited.
- You *earn* every pound lifted or pound lost.
- You *earn* the strength and endurance that makes your hikes feel stronger and easier.

You never get results just because you "want" them. That would be too easy. You get them because you put in the work when it was easier to quit.

The people who understand this lesson are the ones who achieve incredible things—not just in the mountains but in every area of life.

Lesson #2: Growth Is Only on the Other Side of Hard

You will never grow staying inside your comfort zone. You won't get stronger, you won't build muscles, you won't summit mountains, and you certainly won't build resilience. Isn't it funny how we all want resilience but when we're in the midst of the "storm" that builds resilience we seek comfort at all costs instead of choosing to weather the storm? It's ironic when you think about it.

Growth is ultimately the result of overcoming life's storms. It comes from doing hard things well like lifting heavier weights, or doing harder workouts, or tackling longer, challenging days on the trail. It's those hard things that generate growth to raise your floor in life. It's not supposed to be comfortable, it's supposed to make you stronger.

The trail certainly knows how to force you into discomfort to generate that growth.

- When your feet hurt and you still have miles left to go, you learn how to push past pain.
- When you get caught in bad weather and have to adapt, you learn how to stay calm under pressure.
- When you miscalculate a route or get lost in the wilderness and have to problem solve, you learn how to trust yourself in high-stakes situations.

Every challenge on the trail is really just a lesson in adaptability, perseverance, and mental toughness, which are all qualities that separate the strong from the weak.

So if you want to become a stronger, tougher, more resilient version of yourself you have to get comfortable being uncomfortable—physically and mentally. It's going to be hard in the moment, but you'll always be grateful for the growth that comes from it.

Lesson #3: The Mountain's Don't Care About You—and That's a Good Thing

The mountains don't care if you're tired. They don't care what gear you own or how many mountains you've climbed before.

The trailhead is there. The summit is there. Whether you make it or not relies solely on you. You either keep putting one foot in front of the other, or you quit and turn around like I did on Big Slide Mountain. Either way the mountains will remain unphased.

That's the most honest and refreshing reality you'll ever face.

In a world where people expect participation trophies and rewards for half-effort, the mountains remind us of a simple truth:

You don't get what you want. You get what you earn.

This is a hard lesson for some soft people. But once you embrace it, you realize it's actually one of the greatest gifts the mountains give us.

Because if the mountains don't care about your past accomplishments or your current status, it also means they don't hold you back either. The opportunity to do something great is yours for the taking, but it's entirely up to you to take action and start climbing. One foot in front of the other.

No matter who you are, if you put in the full effort, if you respect the challenge, if you show up prepared and keep climbing, the mountains will give you the adventure you're looking for. What an amazing lesson and reflection of real life.

Lesson #4: The Mountains Will Reflect Your Preparation, Good or Bad

The mountains don't lie. They don't care about your excuses, your intentions, or what you *meant* to do before you arrived at the trailhead. They simply reflect the work you either did or didn't do before stepping onto the trail.

The Trail Split: Mindset for the Mountains

Every win and struggle is a direct result of the choices and effort you made long before you laced up your hiking boots.

- If you neglected your physical fitness, the trail will expose that weakness.
- If you got lazy with your prehike homework, the trail will reveal that at the first junction.
- If you aren't prepared with the right gear and equipment, the woods will let you know fast.
- If you haven't built the mental resilience to handle adversity, the first challenge you face will have you ready to quit.

But if you've put in the work—if you've trained consistently, studied the route, and built the discipline to do hard things even when you don't feel like it—the mountains will reward you with the adventure of a lifetime. The journey will always be challenging, sure, but you'll meet that challenge with strength, confidence, and, most importantly, the ability to endure. That last part is key.

The mountains reflect your preparation and your action, plain and simple. No bias. No cares. Just honest reflection.

And once again that's why the mountains are one of life's greatest teachers.

So the next time you train, plan, or push yourself beyond your comfort zone, remember the work you're doing today will determine the kind of adventure you'll have tomorrow. And when you're out on the trail doing hard things well, you're building the strong, resilient person you're meant to become.

Prepare well, and the mountains will always give you a story worth telling.

Lesson #5: Fall in Love with the TRAIL, and the SUMMIT Will Follow

First, let me reword that lesson:

Fall in love with the ~~TRAIL~~ PROCESS, and the ~~SUMMIT~~ RESULTS will follow.

Too many people only focus on the "summit." The end result. The achievement. The moment they stand on top of the world. But if your eyes are only focused on the peak, you'll unfortunately miss the beauty of the trail beneath your feet. Where do you spend more time, on the trail or on the summit?

It's okay, you can answer out loud. "The trail."

The strongest hikers, elite athletes, and the people who achieve great things in life aren't just chasing "summits." They fall in love with the *process* of getting there. They focus on perfecting the work itself. The reps in the gym that lead to the PRs. The trail, the woods, and the climb that takes them to the summit.

We need goals because we need to know where we're heading, but when you fall in love with the process needed to achieve them, those "summits" come as a natural side effect of that pursuit. The mountains teach this lesson better than anything else. So don't just chase the goal but instead aim to fall in love with the process first. The trail is where the real beauty and rewards are found.

Your Five Life Lessons from the Trail

The trail has endless lessons to teach you. The five previous lessons have been profoundly impactful on my own life and how I think, act, and carry myself daily.

Now I ask you: What lessons has the trail taught you? I want you to think about the lessons and write them down here. Yes, actually write them on the paper. Then ask yourself, "Am I applying these lessons to my own life every day?" Bonus points for anyone who emails me to share your life lessons because I want to learn from your lived experiences as well. You can reach me at james@46outdoors.com.

1.
2.
3.
4.
5.

Now that we've done a deep dive into the mindset needed for success in the mountains, which happens to be the same mindset needed for success in life, let's wrap up what you've learned in this book so you can begin having stronger outdoor adventures.

CHAPTER 6

The Final Ascent: Six-Week Training Programs

IN HIKING, THE *FINAL ASCENT* IS THE LAST BIG PUSH TO THE SUMMIT. It's often the steepest, most exposed, and most demanding part of the climb, but it's also the stretch that brings you to the top. The trees thin out, the wind picks up, and every step requires more effort. But when you dig deep and keep climbing, that's when the summit view you've been working for finally reveals itself.

Time to train!

Let's get right down to it. Here are four different battle-tested, ready-to-run training programs to choose from based on your preferences and equipment access. Each program implements the principles you've learned in this book.

In addition to the ready-to-run programs I will also give you plug-and-play templates to build your own training program based on how many days

Push-ups. The basics never go out of style for a reason.

a week you want to train. After coaching hundreds of hikers I've found the five-day-per-week program to be the most optimal, but as you've learned in this book, anything beats nothing every time. The templates include five-day-, four-day-, three-day-, and two-day-per-week options.

PROGRAM RECAP: The Goals and Focus of Each Training Day

Mountain-Strength Day = Strength-focused training with trail-specific conditioning
Elevation Day = Athleticism-focused bodyweight training
Approach Day = Endurance-focused steady-state cardio
Backpack/Ruck Day = Backpack strength, conditioning, and time on your feet

THE FOUR TRAINING PROTOCOLS

The six-week training protocols to choose from are

1. **Barbells and Dumbbells Protocol**
2. Machines-Only Protocol
3. Dumbbells-Only Protocol
4. Bodyweight and Backpack Protocol

Common Training Questions

"How Much Should I Lift?"
There's a difference between "warm-up" weights and "working weights." For the working weights (that is, the three sets of ten reps) you should always choose weights that challenge you for the prescribed rep range. Ideally choose a weight that you can do one to three more reps but no more than that. The goal is to increase the weights week after week. You may need to do a warm-up set or two to prepare your body to use the correct weight. Make sure you're warmed up and ready to go accordingly. Now with that said, don't do a one-quarter rep with heavier weight just to use more weight. Always do the full range of motion even if it means going lighter. Just make sure the weight is always challenging and you're trying to increase it every week.

"Can I Swap Out Equipment?"
Yes. You can change equipment if you prefer (that is, swapping machines for dumbbells, dumbbells for barbells, etc.). Make sure you're training the same muscles in a similar way though.

The Final Ascent: Six-Week Training Programs

"What Should I Do If an Exercise Causes Pain?"
If you need to skip certain movements because of pain, obviously you can do that. Learn to train around the pain accordingly whether that means doing the part of the movement that doesn't hurt, substituting for a similar less painful movement, or if needed switching movements altogether. If that's the case though, swap out lower body for lower body, or upper body for upper body. Just don't swap out shoulder press for a leg extension or a goblet squat for a bench press, for example. Keep it as close as possible and give your best effort.

"I Only Have Light Dumbbells. Will Those Work?"
I want you to build strength. It's time to start lifting heavier weights so you strengthen your muscles, joints, tendons, and ligaments. Light weights for high reps don't do that. Light weights do not "tone" you either. Heavy weights do. In fact, lighter weight for endless reps actually adds *more* wear and tear than heavy weight for fewer reps. So if the program says to do eight to ten reps, for example, but you can do fifteen reps with your weights, then you're not lifting heavy enough to create the training effect we're looking for. It's time to buy heavier weights. If that doesn't work, just lift the weights you have and do as many reps as you can but stop one to two reps shy of muscular failure.

Dumbbell Hack: You can make lighter weights feel heavier and more challenging by slowing down the reps. Lifting ten pounds is one thing, but lifting ten pounds and making it take you ten seconds per rep will be a whole new experience.

"I'm a Beginner and Out of Shape. Will This Program Work for Me?"
Yes. A quality training program will scale with anyone. I've had hundreds of people coming "off the couch" and people with no prior strength training experience have great success. This will push you and challenge you. Stay the course, recognize it's supposed to challenge you, and remind yourself "the mountains are hard too." Revisit the mindset chapter in the book on those hard days when you feel like quitting. You got this!

"I'm Already in Great Shape. Will This Program Work for Me Too?"
Yes. We can always get stronger, faster, and more conditioned. I consider myself to have a decent level of fitness with a 600-plus-pound deadlift, yearly half marathons without training for them, and hiking mountains regularly. These programs help me get stronger and more conditioned and they'll help you. Strength is strength.

"How Do I Gauge My Progress?"
In my years of training and coaching mountain athletes around the country I've found the best indicator for progress is one word: performance. Are you performing better with each workout? Are you increasing your weights and/or reps? Are you feeling more confident in the gym each week? Are you moving faster or for more miles? Are you feeling stronger on the trails? This is how you will properly gauge your progress.

"What Do I Do After This Program?"
You have to keep going. Fitness is a never-ending pursuit. The moment you slow down to "take a break" or stop altogether is the moment you begin backtracking. You're either climbing or sliding, there isn't a third direction with your fitness. That's just the way it is. You'll always need to keep your foot on the gas pedal. It's not always pressed down to the floor necessarily, but you'll always need your foot on the pedal regardless, otherwise you will backtrack. So it's important to play the long game and always challenge yourself to get stronger and fitter. If you want a guide on that journey so you can keep making progress but don't have to do the thinking, my coaching programs will provide that for you like they have for hundreds of others.

OFFICIAL MOUNTAIN-STRENGTH TRAINING PROGRAMS
BARBELL PROTOCOL

Training Split: 5 days a week
Program Duration: 6 weeks
Training Session Durations: 20 to 60 minutes
Total Training Sessions: 30

WEEK 1
Day 1
Mountain-Strength Day 1

1. **Mountain-Strength**
   - Barbell squat: 1 set x 8 to 10 reps
   - Barbell squat: 2 sets x 5 reps. Use same weight as first set.
   - Barbell overhead press: 3 sets x 8 to 10 reps

2. **Elevation Circuit**
   - 3 rounds. 20 seconds of rest between exercises.
     - Dumbbell bench press: 10 reps
     - Dumbbell row: 10 reps
     - Dumbbell biceps curl: 10 reps
3. **Trail Conditioning**
   - Step-ups wearing loaded backpack. Use a 15- to 20-inch box/bench/chair for 60 reps (30/per leg) in 1 set.
4. **Core Finisher**
   - Plank from elbows
     - 2 total minutes. Rest as needed.

Day 2
Elevation Day

- Complete as many rounds as possible (AMRAP): 15 total minutes
  - Bodyweight squats x 10
  - Mountain climbers x 10 (per leg)
  - Push-ups x 10 (modify as needed)
  - Burpees x 5 (modify as needed)
  - Jump lunges x 10 (5 per leg)
  - Rest x 20 seconds

Day 3
Approach Day

- 30 to 60 minutes of steady-state cardio of choice
  - Run, elliptical, bike, stair climber, swim, and so on
  - You can mix and match if you want (that is, 15-minute elliptical + 15-minute bike)
  - Find a challenging pace and maintain it

Day 4
Mountain-Strength Day 2

1. **Mountain-Strength**
   - Bench press: 3 sets x 8 to 10 reps
   - Trap bar deadlift: 3 sets x 8 to 10 reps

2. **Elevation Circuit**
   - 3 rounds. 20 seconds of rest between exercises.
     - Goblet squats: 12 reps
     - Dumbbell Romanian deadlift (RDL): 12 reps
     - Dumbbell lunges: 12 reps (per leg)
3. **Trail Conditioning**
   - Burpees
     - 25 burpees. Find a consistent pace and complete in 1 set.
4. **Core Finisher**
   - Plank from elbows
     - 2 total minutes. Rest as needed.

Day 5
Backpack Day

- Ruck with a loaded backpack for 45 minutes
  - Backpack weight: 20 to 40 pounds
  - Goal: 2.25 miles

WEEK 2
Day 1
Mountain-Strength Day 1

1. **Mountain-Strength**
   - Barbell squat: 1 set x 8 to 10 reps
   - Barbell squat: 2 sets x 6 reps at same weight as first set
   - Barbell overhead press: 4 sets x 8 to 10 reps
2. **Elevation Circuit**
   - 3 rounds. 20 seconds of rest between exercises.
     - Dumbbell incline bench press: 10 reps
     - Dumbbell single-arm row: 10 reps per arm
     - Dumbbell hammer curl: 10 reps
3. **Trail Conditioning**
   - Step-ups wearing loaded backpack
     - Use a 15- to 20-inch box/bench/chair. 110 reps (55/per leg) in 1 set.
4. **Core Finisher**
   - Plank
     - 2 total minutes. Rest as needed.

Day 2
Elevation Day

- Complete 3 rounds as fast as possible. Modify movements if necessary.
    - Burpees x 10 reps
    - Mountain climbers x 20 seconds
    - Squat jumps x 15 reps
    - Mountain climbers x 20 seconds
    - Push-ups x 10 reps
    - Mountain climbers x 20 seconds
    - Jumping jacks x 30 reps
    - Rest 60 seconds

Day 3
Approach Day

- 35 to 60 minutes of steady-state cardio of choice
    - Run, elliptical, bike, stair climber, swim, and so on
    - You can mix and match if you want (that is, 15-minute elliptical + 15-minute bike)
    - Find a challenging pace and maintain it

Day 4
Mountain-Strength Day 2

1. **Mountain-Strength**
    - Bench press: 3 sets x 8 to 10 reps
    - Trap bar deadlift: 2 sets x 8 to 10 reps
        - Lower weight 50% for 1 set of maximum reps
2. **Elevation Circuit**
    - 3 rounds. 20 seconds of rest between exercises.
        - Dumbbell split squats: 12 reps
        - Dumbbell devil's press: 12 reps
        - Dumbbell single-leg calf raises: 20 reps (per leg)
3. **Trail Conditioning**
    - Dumbbell farmer's carry
        - 4 x 40 yards. 45 seconds of rest between sets.
        - Carry 20 to 25% of your bodyweight in each hand

4. **Core Finisher**
   - Plank from elbows
     - 2 total minutes. Rest as needed.

Day 5
Backpack Day + Bonus

- Ruck with a loaded backpack for 45 minutes
  - Backpack weight: 25 to 45 pounds
  - Goal: 2.25 miles
  - BONUS: Complete 15 bodyweight squats wearing your backpack every 5 minutes.

WEEK 3
Day 1
Mountain-Strength Day 1

1. **Mountain-Strength**
   - Barbell squat: 2 sets x 8 to 10 reps
   - Barbell squat: 1 set x 6 reps at same weight as first set
   - Barbell overhead press: 4 sets x 6 to 8 reps (heavier than previous weeks)
2. **Elevation Circuit**
   - 3 rounds. 20 seconds of rest between exercises.
     - Dumbbell chest-supported row: 8 reps
     - Dumbbell incline bench press: 8 reps
     - Dumbbell biceps curl: 12 reps
3. **Trail Conditioning**
   - Step-ups wearing loaded backpack and holding dumbbells
     - Use a 15- to 20-inch box/bench/chair: 80 reps (40/per leg) in 1 set
4. **Core Finisher**
   - 2 rounds
     - Plank: 1 minute
     - Mountain climbers x 20 (per leg)
     - Rest: 1 minute

The Final Ascent: Six-Week Training Programs

Day 2
Elevation Day

- Complete 4 rounds as fast as possible. Modify movements if necessary.
  - 30 jumping jacks
  - 5 push-ups
  - 50 high knees (25 per leg)
  - 7 burpees
  - 50 high knees (25 per leg)
  - 10 jump squats
  - 5 push-ups
  - 10 jump squats
    - 30 mountain climbers
    - 5 push-ups
    - 45-second wall sit
    - Rest 2 minutes

Day 3
Approach Day

- 40 to 60 minutes of steady-state cardio of choice
  - Run, elliptical, bike, stair climber, swim, and so on
  - You can mix and match if you want (that is, 20-minute elliptical + 20-minute bike)
  - Find a challenging pace and maintain it

Day 4
Mountain-Strength Day 2

1. **Mountain-Strength**
   - Bench press: 3 sets x 6 to 8 reps
   - Trap bar deadlift: 2 sets x 6 to 8 reps
     - Lower weight 40% for 1 set of maximum reps
2. **Elevation Circuit**
   - 3 rounds. 20 seconds of rest between exercises
     - Dumbbell step-ups: 12 reps (per leg)
     - Dumbbell single-arm overhead press: 8 reps (per arm)
     - Dumbbell RDL: 12 reps

3. **Trail Conditioning**
   - "10-Second Burpees"
     - Set a timer for 10 minutes. Complete 1 burpee every 10 seconds for 10 minutes. This will be 60 total burpees. Use this as an opportunity to overcome any limiting beliefs. You got this!
4. **Core Finisher**
   - Plank from elbows
     - 2.5 total minutes. Rest as needed.

Day 5
Backpack Day

- Ruck with a loaded backpack for 45 minutes
  - Backpack weight: 25 to 45 pounds
  - Goal: 2.4 miles

WEEK 4
Day 1
Mountain-Strength Day 1

1. **Mountain-Strength**
   - Barbell squat: 3 sets x 8 to 10 reps
   - Barbell squat: Lower weight 50% for 1 set of maximum reps. Your muscles should be burning.
   - Barbell overhead press: 4 x 6 to 8 reps
2. **Elevation Circuit**
   - 3 rounds. 20 seconds of rest between exercises.
     - Dumbbell single-arm row: 12 reps (per arm)
     - Dumbbell incline bench press: 8 reps (heavy)
     - Dumbbell biceps curl: 10 reps
3. **Trail Conditioning**
   - Step-ups wearing loaded backpack and holding dumbbells
     - Use a 15- to 20-inch box/bench/chair: 100 reps (50/per leg) in 1 set
4. **Core Finisher**
   - Plank from elbows
     - 2.5 total minutes. Rest as needed.

Day 2
Elevation Day

- Ladder circuit: Perform 10 reps of each exercise in a circuit, then start over and do 9 reps of each, then 8 reps, . . . 2 reps, 1 rep. Then run the ladder back up.
    - Mountain climbers (per leg)
    - Jumping jacks
    - Jump squats
    - Push-ups
- Modify movements as needed (that is, push-ups from knees, regular squats instead of jumping, etc.)

Day 3
Approach Day

- 40 to 60 minutes of steady-state cardio of choice
    - Run, elliptical, bike, stair climber, swim, and so on
    - You can mix and match if you want (that is, 20-minute elliptical + 20-minute bike)
    - Find a challenging pace and maintain it

Day 4
Mountain-Strength Day 2

1. **Mountain-Strength**
    - Bench press: 4 sets x 6 to 8 reps
    - Trap bar deadlift: 2 sets x 6 to 8 reps
        - Lower weight 30% for 1 set of maximum reps
2. **Elevation Circuit**
    - 3 rounds. 20 seconds of rest between exercises
        - Dumbbell step-ups: 12 reps (per leg)
        - Dumbbell bent over row: 12 reps
        - Dumbbell RDL: 12 reps
3. **Trail Conditioning**
    - Dumbbell farmer's carry
        - 4 x 50 yards. 45 seconds of rest between sets.
        - Carry 25 to 30% of your bodyweight in each hand

4. **Core Finisher**
    - Plank from elbows
        - 2.5 total minutes. Rest as needed.

Day 5
Backpack Carry Day

- Weighted backpack carry: 1 mile *holding* your loaded backpack

Yes. *Carry* your loaded backpack for 1 mile in your arms—do not wear it. Hold it in front of you, or on top of your shoulder, switch positions when needed, and so on.

Whatever you do, do not wear it. This is a grit builder. Have fun.

WEEK 5: TRAIL SPLIT Week
Day 1
Mountain-Strength Day 1

1. **Mountain-Strength**
    - Complete 4 rounds in a circuit. Move at a steady pace, but not a "sprint."
        - Barbell squat: 5 reps (use a weight you can do for 8 to 10 reps)
        - Incline dumbbell bench press: 10 reps
        - Dumbbell chest-supported row: 10 reps
        - Dumbbell shrugs: 20 reps
        - Biceps curls: 12 reps
        - Planks: 30 seconds
        - Rest 2 minutes
2. **Trail Conditioning**
    - 1-mile ruck wearing a loaded backpack *and* carrying dumbbells. Rest as needed.

Day 2
Elevation Day

- Warm-up: 5-minute brisk walk. Maintain a fast pace the entire time.
- Circuit: 4 rounds
    - 40 high knees (20 per leg)
    - 10 burpees
    - 30-second plank

- 10 push-ups
- 6 "backcountry" burpees (3 per leg)*
- 15 jumping jacks
- 30 skater jumps (15 per leg)
- 40 mountain climbers (20 per leg)
- 45-second wall sit
- 90 seconds of rest between rounds

* "Backcountry" burpees are standard burpees with the addition of a box step-up once standing back up. Alternate legs with each rep.

Modify the movements if necessary (that is, squats without the jump, burpees without the push-up, elevated push-ups against a counter, etc.). What matters most is putting in a 100 percent effort and getting the work accomplished.

Day 3
Approach Day

- Weighted carry: 1 mile *holding* loaded backpack

Yup, we're doing it again! Carry your loaded backpack for 1 mile—do not wear it. Hold it in your arms, on top of your shoulder, and so on. You'll know you're doing it right when you're constantly switching your grip throughout the mile.

Remember, this is a grit and real-life strength-building day. Have fun and try to do it faster than last week.

Day 4
Mountain-Strength Day 2

1. **Mountain-Strength**
   - Complete 4 rounds in a circuit. Move at a steady pace, but not a "sprint."
     - Bench press: 5 reps (use a weight you can do for 7 to 8 reps)
     - Dumbbell goblet squats: 15 reps
     - Dumbbell chest-supported row: 10 reps
     - Incline dumbbell bench press: 10 reps
     - Dumbbell RDL: 15 reps

- Dumbbell farmer's carry: carry 35% of your bodyweight in each hand for 30 seconds
- Rest 2 minutes
2. **Trail Conditioning**
  - Step-ups wearing loaded backpack
    - Use a 15- to 20-inch box/bench/chair: 100 reps (50 per leg) in 1 set

Day 5
Backpack Day

- Ruck with a loaded backpack for 45 minutes
  - Backpack weight: 25 to 45 pounds
  - Goal: 2.7 miles

WEEK 6: FINAL ASCENT WEEK
Day 1
Mountain-Strength Day 1

1. **Mountain-Strength Day 1**
   - Barbell squat:
     - Top set: 1 set x 5 to 6 reps (this should be heavy)
     - Back-off set 1: lower the weight 15% for a maximum rep set stopping 1 rep shy of failure
     - Back-off set 2: lower the weight another 10% for a maximum rep set stopping 1 rep shy of failure
     - Barbell overhead press: 5 sets x 5 reps
2. **Elevation Circuit**
   - 3 rounds. 20 seconds of rest between exercises.
     - Dumbbell chest-supported row: 12 reps
     - Dumbbell bench press: 8 reps
     - Dumbbell biceps curls: 10 reps
3. **Trail Conditioning**
   - 30 "backcountry" burpees (alternate legs on step-ups, 15 per leg)
4. **Core Finisher**
   - Plank from elbows
     - 2.5 total minutes. Rest as needed.

Day 2
Elevation Day

- Warm-up: 5-minute brisk walk. Maintain a fast pace the entire time.
- Circuit: tabata day
  - A "tabata" is 8 rounds of "20 seconds work/10 seconds rest."
  - Each tabata lasts 4 total minutes.
  - Example:
    - 0:00–0:20: Exercise (for example, mountain climber)
    - 0:20–0:30: Rest
    - 0:30–0:50: Exercise (for example, mountain climber)
    - 0:50–1:00: Rest
- **Complete 3 different tabatas:** Rest 2 minutes between each tabata.
  - Tabata 1: Burpees
  - Tabata 2: Mountain climbers
  - Tabata 3: Jump squats

Note: Modify the movements if necessary (that is, squats without the jump, burpees without the push-up, etc.). Give it a full effort you're proud of.

Day 3
Approach Day

- 60 minutes of steady-state cardio of choice
  - Run, elliptical, bike, stair climber, swim, and so on
  - You can mix and match if you want (that is, 30-minute elliptical + 30-minute bike)
  - Find a challenging pace and maintain it

Day 4
Mountain-Strength Day 2

1. **Mountain-Strength**
   - Bench press: 5 sets x 5 reps
   - Trap bar deadlift: 2 sets x 5 to 6 reps
     - Back-off set: lower the weight 50% for a maximum rep set stopping 1 rep shy of failure

2. **Elevation Circuit**
   - 3 rounds. 20 seconds of rest between exercises
     - Dumbbell calf raises: 20 reps
     - Dumbbell rows: 12 reps
     - Dumbbell shrugs: 20 reps
3. **Trail Conditioning**
   - Step-ups wearing loaded backpack
     - Use a 15- to 20-inch box/bench/chair: 200 reps (100 per leg) in 1 set. Have fun!
4. **Core Finisher**
   - Plank from elbows
     - 1 max effort set. Push yourself.

Day 5
Pack Test Day
Try to complete one of the **USDA Forest Service Official Pack Tests**. Passing the pack test is a requirement for search and rescue crews, forest firefighters, forest rangers, and more. It's a great challenge to see where you stack and to revisit from time to time for fun and to gauge your progress.

Official USDA Pack Test

- 3-mile ruck on flat terrain
- 45-pound backpack
- Time limit: 45 minutes
- Walking only. No running.

Modified Version
The scaled-down version of this Official Pack Test is

- 2-mile ruck on flat terrain
- 25-pound backpack
- Time limit: 30 minutes
- Walking only. No running.

The first time I ever attempted the Official Pack Test I finished with only fifteen seconds to spare. Yes, literally fifteen seconds. It's hard for a reason. Have fun out there!

MACHINES PROTOCOL

Training Split: 5 days a week
Program Duration: 6 weeks
Training Session Durations: 20 to 60 minutes
Total Training Sessions: 30

WEEK 1
Day 1
Mountain-Strength Day 1

1. **Mountain-Strength**
   - Leg press machine OR hack squat: 1 set x 8 to 10 reps
   - Leg press machine OR hack squat: 2 sets x 5 reps. Use same weight as first set.
   - Shoulder press machine: 3 sets x 8 to 10 reps
2. **Elevation:** Machine-Style Circuit
   - Complete all 3 sets then move to the next machine. 40 seconds of rest between sets.
     - Machine chest press: 3 sets x 10 reps
     - Row or lat pull-down machine: 3 sets x 10 reps
     - Biceps machine: 10 reps
3. **Trail Conditioning**
   - Step-ups wearing loaded backpack
     - Use a 15- to 20-inch box/bench/chair: 60 reps (30 per leg) in 1 set
4. **Core Finisher**
   - Plank from elbows
     - 2 total minutes. Rest as needed.

Day 2
Elevation Day

- Complete as many rounds as possible (AMRAP): 15 total minutes
  - Bodyweight squats x 10
  - Mountain climbers x 10 (per leg)
  - Push-ups x 10 (modify as needed)
  - Burpees x 5 (modify as needed)
  - Jump lunges x 10 (5 per leg)
  - Rest x 20 seconds

Day 3
Approach Day

- 30 to 60 minutes of steady-state cardio of choice
  - Run, elliptical, bike, stair climber, swim, and so on
  - You can mix and match if you want (that is, 15-minute elliptical + 15-minute bike)
  - Find a challenging pace and maintain it

Day 4
Mountain-Strength Day 2

1. **Mountain-Strength**
   - Chest press machine: 3 sets x 8 to 10 reps
   - Single-leg leg press machine: 3 sets x 8 to 10 reps (per leg)
2. **Elevation:** Machine-Style Circuit
   - Complete all 3 sets then move to the next machine. 40 seconds of rest between sets.
     - Leg extension machine: 3 sets x 12 reps
     - Hamstring curl machine: 3 sets x 12 reps
     - Dumbbell or bodyweight lunges: 3 sets x 12 reps (per leg)
3. **Trail Conditioning**
   - Burpees
     - 25 burpees. Find a consistent pace and complete in 1 set.
4. **Core Finisher**
   - Plank from elbows
     - 2 total minutes. Rest as needed.

Day 5
Backpack Day

- Ruck with a loaded backpack for 45 minutes
  - Backpack weight: 20 to 40 pounds
  - Goal: 2.25 miles

WEEK 2
Day 1
Mountain-Strength Day 1

1. **Mountain-Strength**
   - Leg press machine OR hack squat: 1 sets x 8 to 10 reps
   - Leg press machine OR hack squat: 2 sets x 6 reps at same weight as first set
   - Shoulder press machine: 4 sets x 8 to 10 reps
2. **Elevation:** Machine-Style Circuit
   - Complete all 3 sets then move to the next machine. 40 seconds of rest between sets.
     - Chest press machine: 3 sets x 10 reps
     - Lat pull-down machine: 3 sets x 10 reps
     - Biceps curl machine: 3 sets x 10 reps
3. **Trail Conditioning**
   - Step-ups wearing loaded backpack
     - Use a 15- to 20-inch box/bench/chair: 110 reps (55 per leg) in 1 set
4. **Core Finisher**
   - Plank
     - 2 total minutes. Rest as needed.

Day 2
Elevation Day

- Complete 3 rounds as fast as possible. Modify movements if necessary.
  - Burpees x 10 reps
  - Mountain climbers x 20 seconds
  - Squat jumps x 15 reps
  - Mountain climbers x 20 seconds
  - Push-ups x 10 reps
  - Mountain climbers x 20 seconds
  - Jumping jacks x 30 reps
  - Rest 60 seconds

Day 3
Approach Day

- 35 to 60 minutes of steady-state cardio of choice
  - Run, elliptical, bike, stair climber, swim, and so on
  - You can mix and match if you want (that is, 15-minute elliptical + 15-minute bike)
  - Find a challenging pace and maintain it

Day 4
Mountain-Strength Day 2

1. **Mountain-Strength**
   - Chest press machine: 3 sets x 8 to 10 reps
   - Single-leg leg press machine: 2 sets x 8 to 10 reps
     - Lower weight 50% for 1 set of maximum reps
2. **Elevation:** Machine-Style Circuit
   - Complete all 3 sets then move to the next machine. 40 seconds of rest between sets.
     - Leg extension: 3 sets x 12 reps
     - Burpees: 3 sets x 12 reps
     - Single-leg calf raise machine: 3 sets x 20 reps (per leg)
3. **Trail Conditioning**
   - Dumbbell farmer's carry
     - 4 x 40 yards. 45 seconds of rest between sets.
     - Carry 20 to 25% of your bodyweight in each hand
4. **Core Finisher**
   - Plank from elbows
     - 2 total minutes. Rest as needed.

Day 5
Backpack Day + Bonus

- Ruck with a loaded backpack for 45 minutes
  - Backpack weight: 25 to 45 pounds
  - Goal: 2.25 miles
  - BONUS: Complete 15 bodyweight squats wearing your backpack every 5 minutes.

WEEK 3
Day 1
Mountain-Strength Day 1

1. **Mountain-Strength**
   - Leg press machine OR hack squat: 2 sets x 8 to 10 reps
   - Leg press machine OR hack squat: 1 sets x 6 reps at same weight as first set
   - Shoulder press machine: 4 sets x 6 to 8 reps (heavier than previous weeks)
2. **Elevation Circuit**
   - Complete all 3 sets then move to the next machine. 40 seconds of rest between sets.
     - Row machine: 3 sets x 8 reps
     - Incline chest press machine: 3 sets x 8 reps
     - Biceps curl machine or dumbbells: 3 sets x 12 reps
3. **Trail Conditioning**
   - Step-ups wearing loaded backpack and holding dumbbells
     - Use a 15- to 20-inch box/bench/chair: 80 reps (40 per leg) in 1 set
4. **Core Finisher**
   - 2 rounds
     - Plank: 1 minute
     - Mountain climbers x 20 (per leg)
     - Rest: 1 minute

Day 2
Elevation Day

- Complete 4 rounds as fast as possible. Modify movements if necessary.
  - 30 jumping jacks
  - 5 push-ups
  - 50 high knees (25 per leg)
  - 7 burpees
  - 50 high knees (25 per leg)
  - 10 jump squats
  - 5 push-ups
  - 10 jump squats
  - 30 mountain climbers

- 5 push-ups
- 45-second wall sit
- Rest 2 minutes

Day 3
Approach Day

- 40 to 60 minutes of steady-state cardio of choice
  - Run, elliptical, bike, stair climber, swim, and so on
  - You can mix and match if you want (that is, 20-minute elliptical + 20-minute bike)
  - Find a challenging pace and maintain it

Day 4
Mountain-Strength Day 2

1. **Mountain-Strength**
   - Chest press machine: 3 sets x 6 to 8 reps
   - Single-leg leg press machine: 2 sets x 6 to 8 reps per leg
     - Lower weight 40% for 1 set of maximum reps per leg
2. **Elevation Circuit**
   - Complete all 3 sets then move to the next machine. 40 seconds of rest between sets.
     - Dumbbell step-ups: 3 sets x 12 reps (per leg)
     - Row machine: 3 sets x 12 reps
     - Hamstring curl machine: 3 sets x 12 reps
3. **Trail Conditioning**
   - "10-second burpees"
     - Set a timer for 10 minutes. Complete 1 burpee every 10 seconds for 10 minutes. This will be 60 total burpees. Use this as an opportunity to overcome any limiting beliefs. You got this!
4. **Core Finisher**
   - Plank from elbows
     - 2.5 total minutes. Rest as needed.

Day 5
Backpack Day

- Ruck with a loaded backpack for 45 minutes

- Backpack weight: 25 to 45 pounds
- Goal: 2.4 miles

WEEK 4
Day 1
Mountain-Strength 1

1. **Mountain-Strength**
   - Leg press machine OR hack squat: 3 sets x 8 to 10 reps
   - Leg press machine OR hack squat: lower weight 50% for 1 set of maximum reps. Your muscles should be burning.
   - Shoulder press machine: 4 x 6 to 8 reps
2. **Elevation Circuit**
   - Complete all 3 sets then move to the next machine. 40 seconds of rest between sets.
     - Lat pull-down machine: 3 sets x 12 reps
     - Incline chest press machine: 3 sets x 8 reps
     - Biceps curl machine: 3 sets x 10 reps
3. **Trail Conditioning**
   - Step-ups wearing loaded backpack and holding dumbbells
     - Use a 15- to 20-inch box/bench/chair: 110 reps (55 per leg) in 1 set
4. **Core Finisher**
   - Plank from elbows
     - 2.5 total minutes. Rest as needed.

Day 2
Elevation Day

- Ladder circuit: perform 10 reps of each exercise in a circuit, then start over and do 9 reps of each, then 8 reps, . . . 2 reps, 1 rep. Then run the ladder back up.
  - Mountain climbers (per leg)
  - Jumping jacks
  - Jump squats
  - Push-ups
- Modify movements as needed (that is, push-ups from knees, regular squats instead of jumping, etc.)

Day 3
Approach Day

- 40 to 60 minutes of steady-state cardio of choice
  - Run, elliptical, bike, stair climber, swim, and so on
  - You can mix and match if you want (that is, 20-minute elliptical + 20-minute bike)
  - Find a challenging pace and maintain it

Day 4
Mountain-Strength Day2

1. **Mountain-Strength**
   - Chest press machine: 4 sets x 6 to 8 reps
   - Single-leg leg extension machine: 2 sets x 6 to 8 reps per leg
     - Lower weight 30% for 1 set of maximum reps per leg
2. **Elevation Circuit**
   - Complete all 3 sets then move to the next machine. 40 seconds of rest between sets.
     - Leg extension machine: 3 sets x 15 reps
     - Row machine: 3 sets x 12 reps
     - Hamstring curl machine: 3 sets x 10 reps
3. **Trail Conditioning**
   - Dumbbell farmer's carry
     - 4 x 50 yards. 45 seconds of rest between sets.
     - Carry 30 to 35% of your bodyweight in each hand
4. **Core Finisher**
   - Plank from elbows
     - 2.5 total minutes. Rest as needed.

Day 5
Backpack Carry Day

- Weighted backpack carry: 1 mile *holding* your loaded backpack

Yes. *Carry* your loaded backpack for 1 mile in your arms—do not wear it. Hold it in front of you, or on top of your shoulder, switch positions when needed, and so on.

Whatever you do, do not wear it. This is a grit builder. Have fun.

The Final Ascent: Six-Week Training Programs

WEEK 5: TRAIL SPLIT Week
Day 1
Mountain-Strength 1

1. **Mountain-Strength Full-Body Day 1**
   - Complete 4 sets of each movement with only 30 seconds between sets. Maintain a steady pace throughout the workout. We are challenging strength and conditioning at the same time.
     - Leg press machine OR hack squat: 4 sets x 5 reps (use a weight you can do for 8 to 10 reps)
     - Chest press machine: 4 sets x 10 reps
     - Row machine: 4 sets x 10 reps
     - Shoulder press machine: 4 sets x 10 reps
     - Biceps curl machine: 4 sets x 12 reps
     - Planks: 3 sets x 30 seconds
2. **Trail Conditioning**
   - 1-mile ruck wearing a loaded backpack *and* carrying dumbbells. Rest as needed.

Day 2
Elevation Day

- Warm-up: 5-minute brisk walk. Maintain a fast pace the entire time.
- Circuit: 4 rounds
  - 40 high knees (20 per leg)
  - 10 burpees
  - 30-second plank
  - 10 push-ups
  - 6 "backcountry" burpees (3 per leg*)
  - 15 jumping jacks
  - 30 skater jumps (15 per leg)
  - 40 mountain climbers (20 per leg)
  - 45-second wall sit
  - 90 seconds of rest between rounds

* "Backcountry" burpees are standard burpees with the addition of a box step-up once standing back up. Alternate legs with each rep.

Modify the movements if necessary (that is, squats without the jump, burpees without the push-up, elevated push-ups against a counter, etc.).

What matters most is putting in a 100 percent effort and getting the work accomplished.

Day 3
Approach Day

- Weighted carry: 1 mile *holding* loaded backpack

Yup, we're doing it again! Carry your loaded backpack for 1 mile—do not wear it. Hold it in your arms, on top of your shoulder, and so on. You'll know you're doing it right when you're constantly switching your grip throughout the mile.

Remember, this is a grit and real-life strength-building day. Have fun and try to do it faster than last week.

Day 4
Mountain-Strength Day 2

1. **Mountain-Strength Full-Body Day 2**
   - Complete 4 sets of each movement with only 30 seconds between sets. Maintain a steady pace throughout the workout. We are challenging strength and conditioning at the same time.
     - Chest press machine: 4 sets x 5 reps (use a weight you can do for 8 to 10 reps)
     - Leg press machine: 4 sets x 10 reps
     - Lat pull down machine: 4 sets x 10 reps
     - Incline chest press machine: 4 sets x 10 reps
     - Hamstring curl machine: 4 sets x 15 reps
     - Row machine: 4 sets x 10 reps
2. **Trail Conditioning**
   - Step-ups wearing loaded backpack
     - Use a 15- to 20-inch box/bench/chair: 100 reps (50 per leg) in 1 set

Day 5
Backpack Day

- Ruck with a loaded backpack for 45 minutes
  - Backpack weight: 25 to 45 pounds
  - Goal: 2.7 miles

WEEK 6: FINAL ASCENT WEEK
Day 1
Mountain-Strength Day 1

1. **Mountain-Strength Day 1**
   - Leg press machine OR hack squat:
     - Top set: 1 set x 5 to 6 reps (this should be heavy)
     - Back-off set 1: lower the weight 15% for a maximum rep set stopping 1 rep shy of failure
     - Back-off set 2: lower the weight another 10% for a maximum rep set stopping 1 rep shy of failure
     - Shoulder press machine: 5 sets x 5 reps
2. **Elevation Circuit**
   - Complete all 3 sets then move to the next machine. 40 seconds of rest between sets.
     - Row machine: 3 sets x 12 reps
     - Shoulder press machine: 3 sets x 8 reps
     - Biceps curl machine: 3 sets x 10 reps
3. **Trail Conditioning**
   - 30 "backcountry" burpees (alternate legs on step-ups, 15 per leg)
4. **Core Finisher**
   - Plank from elbows
     - 2.5 total minutes. Rest as needed.

Day 2
Elevation Day

- Warm-up: 5-minute brisk walk. Maintain a fast pace the entire time.
- Circuit: tabata day
  - A "tabata" is 8 rounds of "20 seconds work/10 seconds rest."
  - Each tabata lasts 4 total minutes.
  - Example:
    - 0:00–0:20: Exercise (for example, mountain climber)
    - 0:20–0:30: Rest
    - 0:30–0:50: Exercise (for example, mountain climber)
    - 0:50–1:00: Rest

- **Complete 3 different tabatas:** Rest 2 minutes between each tabata.
  - **Tabata 1:** Burpees
  - **Tabata 2:** Mountain climbers
  - **Tabata 3:** Jump squats

Note: Modify the movements if necessary (that is, squats without the jump, burpees without the push-up, etc.). Give it a full effort you're proud of.

Day 3
Approach Day

- 60 minutes of steady-state cardio of choice
  - Run, elliptical, bike, stair climber, swim, and so on
  - You can mix and match if you want (that is, 30-minute elliptical + 30-minute bike)
  - Find a challenging pace and maintain it

Day 4
Mountain-Strength Day 2

1. **Mountain-Strength**
   - Chest press machine: 5 sets x 5 reps
   - Single-leg leg press machine: 2 sets x 5 to 6 reps per leg
     - Back-off set: lower the weight 50% for a maximum rep set stopping 1 rep shy of failure per leg

2. **Elevation Circuit**
   - Complete all 3 sets then move to the next machine. 40 seconds of rest between sets.
     - Calf raise machine: 3 sets x 20 reps
     - Lat pull-down machine: 3 sets x 12 reps
     - Row machine: 3 sets x 20 reps

3. **Trail Conditioning**
   - Step-ups wearing loaded backpack
     - Use a 15- to 20-inch box/bench/chair: 200 reps (100per leg) in 1 set. Have fun!

4. **Core Finisher**
   - Plank from elbows
     - 1 max effort set. Push yourself.

Day 5
Pack Test Day

Try to complete one of the **USDA Forest Service Official Pack Tests**. Passing the pack test is a requirement for search and rescue crews, forest firefighters, forest rangers, and more. It's a great challenge to see where you stack and to revisit from time to time for fun and to gauge your progress.

Official USDA Pack Test:

- 3-mile ruck on flat terrain
- 45-pound backpack
- Time limit: 45 minutes
- Walking only. No running.

Modified Version:
The scaled-down version of this Official Pack Test is

- 2-mile ruck on flat terrain
- 25-pound backpack
- Time limit: 30 minutes
- Walking only. No running.

The first time I ever attempted the Official Pack Test I finished with only fifteen seconds to spare. Yes, literally fifteen seconds. It's hard for a reason. Have fun out there!

DUMBBELLS PROTOCOL
Training Split: 5 days a week
Program Duration: 6 weeks
Training Session Durations: 20 to 60 minutes
Total Training Sessions: 30

WEEK
Day 1
Mountain-Strength Day 1

1. **Mountain-Strength**
   - Dumbbell goblet squat: 3 sets x 10 to 12 reps

- Dumbbell rear foot elevated split squat: 2 sets x 12 reps per leg
- Dumbbell overhead press: 3 sets x 10 to 12 reps

2. **Elevation Circuit**
   - 3 rounds. 20 seconds of rest between exercises.
     - Dumbbell bench press: 10 reps
     - Dumbbell row: 10 reps
     - Dumbbell biceps curl: 10 reps
3. **Trail Conditioning**
   - Step-ups wearing loaded backpack
     - Use a 15- to 20-inch box/bench/chair: 60 reps (30 per leg) in 1 set
4. **Core Finisher**
   - Plank from elbows
     - 2 total minutes. Rest as needed.

Day 2
Elevation Day

- Complete as many rounds as possible (AMRAP): 15 total minutes
  - Bodyweight squats x 10
  - Mountain climbers x 10 (per leg)
  - Push-ups x 10 (modify as needed)
  - Burpees x 5 (modify as needed)
  - Jump lunges x 10 (5 per leg)
  - Rest x 20 seconds

Day 3
Approach Day

- 30 to 60 minutes of steady-state cardio of choice
  - Run, elliptical, bike, stair climber, swim, and so on
  - You can mix and match if you want (that is, 15-minute elliptical + 15-minute bike)
  - Find a challenging pace and maintain it

Day 4
Mountain-Strength Day 2

1. **Mountain-Strength**
   - Dumbbell bench press: 3 sets x 10 to 12 reps

- Dumbbell RDL: 3 sets x 10 to 12 reps
2. **Elevation Circuit**
    - 3 rounds. 20 seconds of rest between exercises
        - Goblet squats: 12 reps
        - Dumbbell Romanian deadlift (RDL): 12 reps
        - Dumbbell lunges: 12 reps (per leg)
3. **Trail Conditioning**
    - Burpees
        - 25 burpees. Find a consistent pace and complete in 1 set.
4. **Core Finisher**
    - Plank from elbows
        - 2 total minutes. Rest as needed.

Day 5
Backpack Day

- Ruck with a loaded backpack for 45 minutes
    - Backpack weight: 20 to 40 pounds
    - Goal: 2.25 miles

WEEK 2
Day 1
Mountain-Strength Day 1

1. **Mountain-Strength**
    - Dumbbell goblet squat: 3 sets x 8 to 10 reps
    - Dumbbell rear foot elevated split squat: 2 sets x 10 to 12 reps per leg. Increase dumbbell weights from previous week.
    - Dumbbell overhead press: 4 sets x 8 to 10 reps
2. **Elevation Circuit**
    - 3 rounds. 20 seconds of rest between exercises.
        - Dumbbell incline bench press: 10 reps
        - Dumbbell single-arm row: 10 reps per arm
        - Dumbbell hammer curl: 10 reps
3.) **Trail Conditioning**
    - Step-ups wearing loaded backpack
        - Use a 15- to 20-inch box/bench/chair: 110 reps (55 per leg) in 1 set

4. **Core Finisher**
   - Plank
     - 2 total minutes. Rest as needed.

Day 2
Elevation Day

- Complete 3 rounds as fast as possible. Modify movements if necessary.
  - Burpees x 10 reps
  - Mountain climbers x 20 seconds
  - Squat jumps x 15 reps
  - Mountain climbers x 20 seconds
  - Push-ups x 10 reps
  - Mountain climbers x 20 seconds
  - Jumping jacks x 30 reps
  - Rest 60 seconds

Day 3
Approach Day

- 35 to 60 minutes of steady-state cardio of choice
  - Run, elliptical, bike, stair climber, swim, and so on
  - You can mix and match if you want (that is, 15-minute elliptical + 15-minute bike)
  - Find a challenging pace and maintain it

Day 4
Mountain-Strength Day 2

1. **Mountain-Strength**
   - Dumbbell bench press: 4 sets x 8 to 10 reps
   - Dumbbell RDL: 4 sets x 8 to 10 reps. Take 3 seconds on the way down (eccentric).
     - Lower weight 50% for 1 set of maximum reps
2. **Elevation Circuit**
   - 3 rounds. 20 seconds of rest between exercises
     - Dumbbell split squats: 12 reps
     - Dumbbell devil's press: 12 reps
     - Dumbbell single-leg calf raises: 20 reps (per leg)

3. **Trail Conditioning**
   - Dumbbell farmer's carry
     - 4 x 40 yards. 45 seconds of rest between sets.
     - Carry 20 to 25% of your bodyweight in each hand
4.) **Core Finisher**
   - Plank from elbows
     - 2 total minutes. Rest as needed.

Day 5
Backpack Day + Bonus

- Ruck with a loaded backpack for 45 minutes
  - Backpack weight: 25 to 45 pounds
  - Goal: 2.25 miles
  - BONUS: Complete 15 bodyweight squats wearing your backpack every 5 minutes.

WEEK 3
Day 1
Mountain-Strength 1

1. **Mountain-Strength**
   - Dumbbell goblet squat: 3 sets x 8 to 10 reps. Take 3 seconds on the way down (eccentric).
   - Dumbbell rear foot elevated split squat: 3 sets x 10 per leg. Increase dumbbell weights from previous week.
   - Dumbbell overhead press: 4 sets x 6 to 8 reps (heavier than previous week)
2. **Elevation Circuit**
   - 3 rounds. 20 seconds of rest between exercises.
     - Dumbbell chest supported row: 8 to 10 reps
     - Dumbbell incline bench press: 8 to 10 reps
     - Dumbbell biceps curl: 12 reps
3. **Trail Conditioning**
   - Step-ups wearing loaded backpack and holding dumbbells
     - Use a 15- to 20-inch box/bench/chair: 80 reps (40 per leg) in 1 set
4. **Core Finisher**
   - 2 rounds

- Plank: 1 minute
- Mountain climbers x 20 (per leg)
- Rest: 1 minute

Day 2
Elevation Day

- Complete 4 rounds as fast as possible. Modify movements if necessary.
  - 30 jumping jacks
  - 5 push-ups
  - 50 high knees (25 per leg)
  - 7 burpees
  - 50 high knees (25 per leg)
  - 10 jump squats
  - 5 push-ups
  - 10 jump squats
  - 30 mountain climbers
  - 5 push-ups
  - 45-second wall sit
  - Rest 2 minutes

Day 3
Approach Day

- 40 to 60 minutes of steady-state cardio of choice
  - Run, elliptical, bike, stair climber, swim, and so on
  - You can mix and match if you want (that is, 20-minute elliptical + 20-minute bike)
  - Find a challenging pace and maintain it

Day 4
Mountain-Strength 2

1. **Mountain-Strength**
   - Dumbbell bench press: 4 sets x 6 to 8 reps
   - Dumbbell RDL: 4 sets x 8 to 10 reps. Take 3 seconds on the way down (eccentric).
     - Lower weight 40% for 1 set of maximum reps

2. **Elevation Circuit**
   - 3 rounds. 20 seconds of rest between exercises.
     - Dumbbell step-ups: 12 reps (per leg)
     - Dumbbell bent over row: 12 reps
     - Dumbbell single-arm shoulder press: 8 reps (per arm)
3. **Trail Conditioning**
   - "10 second burpees"
     - Set a timer for 10 minutes. Complete 1 burpee every 10 seconds for 10 minutes. This will be 60 total burpees. Use this as an opportunity to overcome any limiting beliefs. You got this!
4. **Core Finisher**
   - Plank from elbows
     - 2.5 total minutes. Rest as needed.

Day 5
Backpack Day

- Ruck with a loaded backpack for 45 minutes
  - Backpack weight: 25 to 45 pounds
  - Goal: 2.4 miles

WEEK 4
Day 1
Mountain-Strength Day 1

1. **Mountain-Strength**
   - Dumbbell front squat: 3 sets x 8 to 10 reps
   - Dumbbell rear foot elevated split squat: 3 x 10 per leg
   - Dumbbell single-arm overhead press: 4 x 6 to 8 reps per arm
2. **Elevation Circuit**
   - 3 rounds. 20 seconds of rest between exercises.
     - Dumbbell single-arm row: 12 reps (per arm)
     - Dumbbell incline bench press: 6 to 8 reps (heavy)
     - Dumbbell biceps curl: 10 reps
3. **Trail Conditioning**
   - Step-ups wearing loaded backpack and holding dumbbells
     - Use a 15- to 20-inch box/bench/chair: 110 reps (55 per leg) in 1 set

4. **Core Finisher**
   - Plank from elbows
     - 2.5 total minutes. Rest as needed.

Day 2
Elevation Day

- Ladder circuit: perform 10 reps of each exercise in a circuit, then start over and do 9 reps of each, then 8 reps, . . . 2 reps, 1 rep. Then run the ladder back up.
  - Mountain climbers (per leg)
  - Jumping jacks
  - Jump squats
  - Push-ups
- Modify movements as needed (that is, push-ups from knees, regular squats instead of jumping, etc.)

Day 3
Approach Day

- 40 to 60 minutes of steady-state cardio of choice
  - Run, elliptical, bike, stair climber, swim, and so on
  - You can mix and match if you want (that is, 20-minute elliptical + 20-minute bike)
  - Find a challenging pace and maintain it

Day 4
Mountain-Strength Day 2

1. **Mountain-Strength**
   - Dumbbell bench press: 4 sets x 6 to 8 reps
   - Dumbbell RDL: 4 sets x 8 to 10 reps. Take 3 seconds on the way down (eccentric).
     - Lower weight 20% for 1 set of maximum reps
2. **Elevation Circuit**
   - 3 rounds. 20 seconds of rest between exercises
     - Dumbbell step-ups: 12 reps (per leg)
     - Dumbbell bent over row: 12 reps
     - Dumbbell single-arm shoulder press: 12 reps per arm

The Final Ascent: Six-Week Training Programs

3. **Trail Conditioning**
   - Dumbbell farmer's carry
     - 4 x 50 yards. 45 seconds of rest between sets.
     - Carry 25% of your bodyweight in each hand
4. **Core Finisher**
   - Plank from elbows
     - 2.5 total minutes. Rest as needed.

Day 5
Backpack Carry Day

- Weighted backpack carry: 1 mile *holding* your loaded backpack.

Yes. *Carry* your loaded backpack for 1 mile in your arms—do not wear it. Hold it in front of you, or on top of your shoulder, switch positions when needed, etc.

Whatever you do, do not wear it. This is a grit builder. Have fun.

WEEK 5: TRAIL SPLIT Week
Day 1
Mountain-Strength Day 1

1. **Mountain-Strength Circuit**
   - Complete 4 rounds in a circuit. Move at a steady pace, but not a "sprint."
     - Dumbbell front squat: 10 reps
     - Incline dumbbell bench press: 10 reps
     - Dumbbell chest-supported row: 10 reps
     - Dumbbell shrugs: 20 reps
     - Biceps curls: 12 rep
     - Planks: 30 seconds
     - Rest 2 minutes
2. **Trail Conditioning**
   - 1-mile ruck wearing a loaded backpack *and* carrying dumbbells. Rest as needed.

Day 2
Elevation Day

- Warm-up: 5-minute brisk walk. Maintain a fast pace the entire time.

- Circuit: 4 rounds
    - 40 high knees (20 per leg)
    - 10 burpees
    - 30-second plank
    - 10 push-ups
    - 6 "backcountry" burpees (3 per leg*)
    - 15 jumping jacks
    - 30 skater jumps (15 per leg)
    - 40 mountain climbers (20 per leg)
    - 45-second wall sit
    - 90 seconds of rest between rounds

* "Backcountry" burpees are standard burpees with the addition of a box step-up once standing back up. Alternate legs with each rep.

Modify the movements if necessary (that is, squats without the jump, burpees without the push-up, elevated push-ups against a counter, etc.). What matters most is putting in a 100 percent effort and getting the work accomplished.

Day 3
Approach Day

- Weighted backpack carry: 1 mile *holding* loaded backpack

Yup, we're doing it again! Carry your loaded backpack for 1 mile—do not wear it. Hold it in your arms, on top of your shoulder, etc. You'll know you're doing it right when you're constantly switching your grip throughout the mile.

Remember, this is a grit and real-life strength-building day. Have fun and try to do it faster than last week.

Day 4
Mountain-Strength Day 2

1. **Mountain-Strength**
    - Complete 4 rounds in a circuit. Move at a steady pace, but not a "sprint."
        - Dumbbell bench press: 8 reps

- Dumbbell goblet squats: 15 reps
- Dumbbell chest-supported row: 10 reps
- Incline dumbbell bench press: 10 reps
- Dumbbell RDL: 15 reps
- Dumbbell farmer's carry: carry 35% of your bodyweight in each hand for 30 seconds
- Rest 2 minutes
2. **Trail Conditioning**
    - Step-ups wearing loaded backpack
        - Use a 15- to 20-inch box/bench/chair: 100 reps (50 per leg) in 1 set

Day 5
Backpack Day

- Ruck with a loaded backpack for 45 minutes
    - Backpack weight: 25 to 45 pounds
    - Goal: 2.7 miles

WEEK 6: FINAL ASCENT WEEK
Day 1
Mountain-Strength Day 1

1. **Mountain-Strength Day 1**
    - Superset: 10 sets x 10 reps each. 30 seconds of rest between supersets.
    - Dumbbell front squat and dumbbell overhead press
2. **Elevation Circuit**
    - Choose a weight you would do in the 10 to 12 rep range for each movement. Then complete 50 reps of each exercise as fast as possible in a circuit. Keep rest times under 20 seconds. This should challenge you.
        - Dumbbell chest-supported row
        - Dumbbell bench press
        - Dumbbell biceps curls
3. **Trail Conditioning**
    - 30 "backcountry" burpees (alternate legs on step-ups, 15 per leg)
4. **Core Finisher**
    - Plank from elbows
        - 2.5 total minutes. Rest as needed.

Day 2:
Elevation Day

- Warm-up: 5-minute brisk walk. Maintain a fast pace the entire time.
- Circuit: tabata day
  - A "tabata" is 8 rounds of "20 seconds work/10 seconds rest."
  - Each tabata lasts 4 total minutes.
  - Example:
    - 0:00–0:20: Exercise (for example, mountain climber)
    - 0:20–0:30: Rest
    - 0:30–0:50: Exercise (for example, mountain climber)
    - 0:50–1:00: Rest
  - **Complete 3 different tabatas:** Rest 2 minutes between each tabata.
    - Tabata 1: Burpees
    - Tabata 2: Mountain climbers
    - Tabata 3: Jump squats

Note: Modify the movements if necessary (that is, squats without the jump, burpees without the push-up, etc.). Give it a full effort you're proud of.

Day 3
Approach Day

- 60 minutes of steady-state cardio of choice
  - Run, elliptical, bike, stair climber, swim, and so on
  - You can mix and match if you want (that is, 30-minute elliptical + 30-minute bike)
  - Find a challenging pace and maintain it

Day 4
Mountain-Strength Day 2

1. **Mountain-Strength**
   - Superset: 5 sets x 10 reps each. 30 seconds of rest between supersets.
   - Dumbbell bench press and dumbbell chest-supported rows
2. **Elevation Circuit**
   - Choose a weight you would do in the 10 to 12 rep range for each movement. Then complete 50 reps of each exercise as fast as possible in a circuit. Keep rest times under 20 seconds. This should challenge you.

- Dumbbell RDL
- Dumbbell calf raises
- Dumbbell shrugs

3. **Trail Conditioning**
   - Step-ups wearing loaded backpack
     - Use a 15- to 20-inch box/bench/chair: 200 reps (100 per leg) in 1 set. Have fun!

4. **Core Finisher**
   - Plank from elbows
     - 1 max effort set. Push yourself.

Day 5
Pack Test Day

Try to complete one of the **USDA Forest Service Official Pack Tests**. Passing the pack test is a requirement for search and rescue crews, forest firefighters, forest rangers, and more. It's a great challenge to see where you stack and to revisit from time to time for fun and to gauge your progress.

Official USDA Pack Test:

- 3-mile ruck on flat terrain
- 45-pound backpack
- Time limit: 45 minutes
- Walking only. No running.

Modified Version:

The scaled-down version of this Official Pack Test is

- 2-mile ruck on flat terrain
- 25-pound backpack
- Time limit: 30 minutes
- Walking only. No running.

The first time I ever attempted the Official Pack Test I finished with only fifteen seconds to spare. Yes, literally fifteen seconds. It's hard for a reason. Have fun out there!

BODYWEIGHT AND BACKPACK PROTOCOL

Training Split: 5 days a week
Program Duration: 6 weeks
Training Session Durations: 20 to 60 minutes
Total Training Sessions: 30

WEEK 1
Day 1
Mountain-Strength Day 1

1. **Mountain-Strength**
   - Circuit: 4 rounds
     - "10-second" bodyweight squats x 10 reps (5 seconds down, 5 seconds up)
     - Mountain climbers x 30 seconds
     - 60 seconds of rest
2. **Elevation Circuit**
   - 4 rounds. Wearing loaded backpack.
     - Rear foot elevated split squat x 12 per leg
     - Walking lunges x 12 steps per leg
     - Push-ups x 12 (modify if necessary)
3. **Trail Conditioning**
   - Burpees
     - 25 reps. Find a steady pace and stick to it for 25 reps.
4. **Core Finisher**
   - Plank from elbows
     - 2 total minutes. Rest as needed.

Day 2
Elevation Day

- Complete as many rounds as possible (AMRAP): 15 total minutes
  - Bodyweight squats x 10
  - Mountain climbers x 10 (per leg)
  - Push-ups x 10 (modify as needed)
  - Burpees x 5 (modify as needed)
  - Jump lunges x 10 (5 per leg)
  - Rest x 20 seconds

Day 3
Approach Day

- 30 to 60 minutes of steady-state cardio of choice
  - Run, elliptical, bike, stair climber, swim, and so on
  - You can mix and match if you want (that is, 15-minute elliptical + 15-minute bike)
  - Find a challenging pace and maintain it

Day 4
Mountain-Strength Day 2

1. **Mountain-Strength**
   - 10 rounds of the "Gothics Strength Protocol"
     - Push-ups
     - Jump squats
   - How to complete the "Gothics Strength Protocol": perform exercise one (that is, push-ups) for 30 seconds, then rest for 30 seconds. Next complete exercise two (that is, jump squats) for 30 seconds, then rest for 30 seconds. Then back to exercise one and so on. Set a timer for 20 minutes and complete the 10 rounds.
2. **Elevation Circuit**
   - 4 rounds. 20 seconds of rest between exercises. Hold your loaded backpack in your arms for each exercise. Do not wear it.
     - Goblet squats: 12 reps
     - Dumbbell Romanian deadlift (RDL): 12 reps
     - Dumbbell lunges: 12 reps (per leg)
3. **Trail Conditioning**
   - Step-ups wearing loaded backpack
     - Use a 15- to 20-inch box/bench/chair: 60 reps (30 per leg) in 1 set
4. **Core Finisher**
   - Plank from elbows
     - 2 total minutes. Rest as needed.

Day 5
Backpack Day

- Ruck with a loaded backpack for 45 minutes

- Backpack weight: 20 to 40 pounds
- Goal: 2.25 miles

WEEK 2
Day 1
Mountain-Strength Day 1

1. **Mountain-Strength**
   - "1.5" squats x 15 (Squat down, stand up only half way, then drop back down, then stand fully up. That is 1 rep. Therefore every rep is actually 1.5 reps.)
   - Mountain climbers x 20 seconds
   - 60 seconds of rest
2. **Elevation Circuit**
   - 3 rounds. 20 seconds of rest between exercises.
     - Jump squats: 10 reps
     - Push-ups: 15 reps (modify if needed)
     - Plank: 30 seconds
     - Burpees: 10 reps
3. **Trail Conditioning**
   - Walking lunges wearing loaded hiking backpack
     - 60 total steps (30 per leg)
4. **Core Finisher**
   - Plank
     - 2 total minutes. Rest as needed.

Day 2
Elevation Day

- Complete 3 rounds as fast as possible. Modify movements if necessary.
  - Burpees x 10 reps
  - Mountain climbers x 20 seconds
  - Squat jumps x 15 reps
  - Mountain climbers x 20 seconds
  - Push-ups x 10 reps
  - Mountain climbers x 20 seconds
  - Jumping jacks x 30 reps
  - Rest 60 seconds

Day 3
Approach Day

- 35 to 60 minutes of steady-state cardio of choice
  - Run, elliptical, bike, stair climber, swim, and so on
  - You can mix and match if you want (that is, 15-minute elliptical + 15-minute bike)
  - Find a challenging pace and maintain it

Day 4
Mountain-Strength Day 2

1. **Mountain-Strength**
   - 10 rounds of the "Gothics Strength Protocol"
     - "Jester" squats (bear hug loaded backpack and squat)
     - "Jester" press (Use loaded backpack: lift backpack from the floor to overhead and back to the floor again. That's 1 rep.)
   - How to complete the "Gothics Strength Protocol": perform exercise one (that is, "jester" squats) for 30 seconds, then rest for 30 seconds. Next complete exercise two (that is, "jester" press) for 30 seconds, then rest for 30 seconds. Then back to exercise one and so on. Set a timer for 20 minutes and complete the 10 rounds.
2. **Elevation Circuit**
   - 4 rounds. 20 seconds of rest between exercises. Wear a loaded backpack.
     - Squats: 12 reps
     - Dumbbell Romanian deadlift (RDL): 12 reps
     - Walking lunges: 12 reps (per leg)
3. **Trail Conditioning**
   - "Backcountry" burpees
     - 30 reps (15 per leg). Alternate legs on each step-up.
4. **Core Finisher**
   - Plank from elbows
     - 2 total minutes. Rest as needed.

Day 5
Backpack Day + Bonus

- Ruck with a loaded backpack for 45 minutes

- Backpack weight: 25 to 45 pounds
- Goal: 2.25 miles
- BONUS: Complete 15 bodyweight squats wearing your backpack every 5 minutes.

WEEK 3
Day 1
Mountain-Strength Day 1

1. **Mountain-Strength**
   - Circuit: 4 rounds
     - "10-second" bodyweight squats x 12 reps (5 seconds down, 5 seconds up)
     - Mountain climbers x 30 seconds
     - 45 seconds of rest
2. **Elevation Circuit**
   - 4 rounds. 20 seconds of rest between exercises. Wear a loaded backpack.
     - Push-ups: 12 reps
     - Side lunges: 12 reps per leg
     - Calf raises: 50 reps
3. **Trail Conditioning**
   - Step-ups wearing loaded backpack
     - Use a 15- to 20-inch box/bench/chair: 80 reps (40 per leg) in 1 set
4. **Core Finisher**
   - 2 rounds
     - Plank: 1 minute
     - Mountain climbers x 20 (per leg)
     - Rest: 1 minute

Day 2
Elevation Day

- Complete 4 rounds as fast as possible. Modify movements if necessary.
  - 30 jumping jacks
  - 5 push-ups
  - 50 high knees (25 per leg)

- 7 burpees
- 50 high knees (25 per leg)
- 10 jump squats
- 5 push-ups
- 10 jump squats
- 30 mountain climbers
- 5 push-ups
- 45-second wall sit
- Rest 2 minutes

Day 3
Approach Day

- 40 to 60 minutes of steady-state cardio of choice
  - Run, elliptical, bike, stair climber, swim, and so on
  - You can mix and match if you want (that is, 20-minute elliptical + 20-minute bike)
  - Find a challenging pace and maintain it

Day 4
Mountain-Strength Day 2

1. **Mountain-Strength**
   - 4 rounds. Modify movements if needed.
     - Rear foot elevated split squats holding backpack on shoulder x 10 reps per leg
     - Push-ups x 15 reps
2. **Elevation Circuit**
   - 4 rounds. 20 seconds of rest between exercises.
     - "Jester" press x 12 reps
     - RDL x 12 reps
     - "Jester" lunge and press x 12 reps per leg
   - "Jester" lunge and press: hold a backpack in front of you, perform a lunge, then at the bottom of each lunge press the pack over your head, then stand back up. Your whole body will be working together during this movement.
3. **Trail Conditioning**
   - "10-second burpees"

- Set a timer for 10 minutes. Complete 1 burpee every 10 seconds for 10 minutes. This will be 60 total burpees. Use this as an opportunity to overcome any limiting beliefs. You got this!

4. **Core Finisher**
   - Plank from elbows
     - 2.5 total minutes. Rest as needed.

Day 5
Backpack Day

- Ruck with a loaded backpack for 45 minutes
  - Backpack weight: 25 to 45 pounds
  - Goal: 2.4 miles

WEEK 4
Day 1
Mountain-Strength Day 1

1. **Mountain-Strength**
   - "1.5" squats x 12 reps (Squat down, stand up only half way, then drop back down, then stand fully up. That is 1 rep. Therefore every rep is actually 1.5 reps.)
   - Burpees x 5 reps
   - Mountain climbers x 20 seconds
   - 60 seconds of rest
2. **Elevation Circuit**
   - 3 rounds. 20 seconds of rest between exercises.
     - Push-ups x 15 reps
     - "Jester" squats x 15 reps
     - Flutter kicks x 30 (15 per leg)
     - "Jester" lunge and press x 20 (10 per leg)
3. **Trail Conditioning**
   - 1-mile jog or do a fast ruck wearing a heavy backpack
4. **Core Finisher**
   - Plank from elbows
     - 2.5 total minutes. Rest as needed.

Day 2
Elevation Day

- Ladder circuit: perform 10 reps of each exercise in a circuit, then start over and do 9 reps of each, then 8 reps, . . . 2 reps, 1 rep. Then run the ladder back up.
    - Mountain climbers (per leg)
    - Jumping jacks
    - Jump squats
    - Push-ups
- Modify movements as needed (that is, push-ups from knees, regular squats instead of jumping, etc.)

Day 3
Approach Day

- 40 to 60 minutes of steady-state cardio of choice
    - Run, elliptical, bike, stair climber, swim, and so on
    - You can mix and match if you want (that is, 20-minute elliptical + 20-minute bike)
    - Find a challenging pace and maintain it

Day 4
Mountain-Strength Day 2

1. **Mountain-Strength**
   - 10 rounds of the "Gothics Strength Protocol"
       - Push-ups (modify if needed)
       - "Jester" lunge and press
   - How to complete the "Gothics Strength Protocol": perform exercise one (that is, push-ups) for 30 seconds, then rest for 30 seconds. Next complete exercise two (that is, "jester" lunge and press) for 30 seconds, then rest for 30 seconds. Then back to exercise one and so on. Set a timer for 20 minutes and complete the 10 rounds.
2. **Elevation Circuit**
   - 4 rounds. 20 seconds of rest between exercises. Wear a loaded backpack.
       - Side lunges x 12 reps (per leg)

- RDLs x 15 reps
- Squats x 20 reps
3. **Trail Conditioning**
    - Step-ups holding a loaded backpack. "Bear hug" your backpack in front of you.
        - Use a 15- to 20-inch box/bench/chair: 80 reps (40 per leg) in 1 set
4. **Core Finisher**
    - Plank from elbows
        - 2.5 total minutes. Rest as needed.

Day 5
Backpack Carry Day

- Weighted backpack carry: 1 mile *holding* your loaded backpack.

Yes. *Carry* your loaded backpack for 1 mile in your arms—do not wear it. Hold it in front of you, or on top of your shoulder, switch positions when needed, etc.

Whatever you do, do not wear it. This is a grit builder. Have fun.

WEEK 5: TRAIL SPLIT Week
Day 1
Mountain-Strength Day 1

1. **Mountain-Strength**
    - Complete 100 reps of each exercise as quickly as possible
        - Jump squats
        - Mountain climbers (100 per leg)
        - Push-ups (modify if needed)
        - Calf raises
        - Lunges (100 per leg)
2. **Trail Conditioning**
    - 1-mile ruck wearing a loaded backpack

Day 2
Elevation Day

- Warm-up: 5-minute brisk walk. Maintain a fast pace the entire time.

- Circuit: 4 rounds
    - 40 high knees (20 per leg)
    - 10 burpees
    - 30-second plank
    - 10 push-ups
    - 6 "backcountry" burpees (3 per leg*)
    - 15 jumping jacks
    - 30 skater jumps (15 per leg)
    - 40 mountain climbers (20 per leg)
    - 45-second wall sit
    - 90 seconds of rest between rounds

* "Backcountry" burpees are standard burpees with the addition of a box step-up once standing back up. Alternate legs with each rep.

Modify the movements if necessary (that is, squats without the jump, burpees without the push-up, elevated push-ups against a counter, etc.). What matters most is putting in a 100 percent effort and getting the work accomplished.

Day 3
Approach Day

- Weighted carry: 1 mile *holding* loaded backpack

Yup, we're doing it again! Carry your loaded backpack for 1 mile—do not wear it. Hold it in your arms, on top of your shoulder, and so on. You'll know you're doing it right when you're constantly switching your grip throughout the mile.

Remember, this is a grit and real-life strength-building day. Have fun and try to do it faster than last week.

Day 4
Mountain-Strength Day 2

1. **Mountain-Strength**
    - Complete 100 reps of each exercise as quickly as possible
        - Burpees
        - Yup. That's it . . . just burpees. Have "fun."

2. **Trail Conditioning**
   - Step-ups wearing loaded backpack
     - Use a 15- to 20-inch box/bench/chair: 100 reps (50 per leg) in 1 set

Day 5
Backpack Day

- Ruck with a loaded backpack for 45 minutes
  - Backpack weight: 25 to 45 pounds
  - Goal: 2.7 miles

WEEK 6: FINAL ASCENT WEEK
Day 1
Mountain-Strength 1
Mountain-Strength Day 1

1. **Mountain-Strength**
   - Circuit: 4 rounds
     - "10-second" bodyweight squats x 12 reps (5 seconds down, 5 seconds up)
     - Mountain climbers x 30 seconds
     - 30 seconds of rest
2. **Elevation Circuit**
   - 4 rounds. Wearing loaded backpack.
     - Rear foot elevated split squat x 12 per leg
     - Walking lunges x 12 steps per leg
     - Push-ups x 12 (modify if necessary)
3. **Trail Conditioning**
   - "Backcountry" burpees
     - 30 "backcountry" burpees (alternate legs on step-ups, 15 per leg)
4. **Core Finisher**
   - Plank from elbows
     - 2 total minutes. Rest as needed.

Day 2
Elevation Day

- Warm-up: 5-minute brisk walk. Maintain a fast pace the entire time.
- Circuit: tabata day

- A "tabata" is 8 rounds of "20 seconds work/10 seconds rest."
- Each tabata lasts 4 total minutes.
- Example:
  - 0:00–0:20: Exercise (for example, mountain climber)
  - 0:20–0:30: Rest
  - 0:30–0:50: Exercise (for example, mountain climber)
  - 0:50–1:00: Rest
- **Complete 3 different tabatas:** Rest 2 minutes between each tabata.
  - Tabata 1: Burpees
  - Tabata 2: Mountain climbers
  - Tabata 3: Jump squats

Note: Modify the movements if necessary (that is, squats without the jump, burpees without the push-up, etc.). Give it a full effort you're proud of.

Day 3
Approach Day

- 60 minutes of steady-state cardio of choice
  - Run, elliptical, bike, stair climber, swim, and so on
  - You can mix and match if you want (that is, 30-minute elliptical + 30-minute bike)
  - Find a challenging pace and maintain it

Day 4
Mountain-Strength Day 2

1. **Mountain-Strength:**
   - 4 rounds. 20 seconds of rest between exercises.
     - "Jester" press x 12 reps
     - RDL x 12 reps
     - "Jester" lunge and press x 12 reps per leg
   - "Jester" lunge and press: hold a backpack in front of you, perform a lunge, then at the bottom of each lunge press the pack over your head, then stand back up. Your whole body will be working together during this movement.
2. **Elevation Circuit**
   - 4 rounds. 20 seconds of rest between exercises. Wear a loaded backpack.

- Push-ups: 12 reps
- Calf raises: 50 reps
- Squats: 15 reps

3. **Trail Conditioning**
   - Step-ups wearing loaded backpack
     - Use a 15- to 20-inch box/bench/chair: 200 reps (100 per leg) in 1 set. Have fun!
4. **Core Finisher**
   - Plank from elbows
     - 1 max effort set. Push yourself.

Day 5
Pack Test Day

Try to complete one of the **USDA Forest Service Official Pack Tests**. Passing the pack test is a requirement for search and rescue crews, forest firefighters, forest rangers, and more. It's a great challenge to see where you stack and to revisit from time to time for fun and to gauge your progress.

Official USDA Pack Test

- 3-mile ruck on flat terrain
- 45-pound backpack
- Time limit: 45 minutes
- Walking only. No running.

Modified Version:
The scaled-down version of this Official Pack Test is

- 2-mile ruck on flat terrain
- 25-pound backpack
- Time limit: 30 minutes
- Walking only. No running.

The first time I ever attempted the Official Pack Test I finished with only fifteen seconds to spare. Yes, literally fifteen seconds. It's hard for a reason. Have fun out there!

The Final Ascent: Six-Week Training Programs

DIY Training Templates
Here is a blueprint for you to plug and play to build your own training programs based on the number of days per week you want to train.

FIVE-DAY TRAINING SPLIT

- x 2 Mountain-Strength Days
- x 1 Elevation Day
- x 1 Approach Day
- x 1 Backpack/Ruck/Hike Day

FIVE-DAY TEMPLATE

- **Day 1**
- **Mountain-Strength 1**
- **(Lower Body Strength + Full Body Grind Circuit)**
  - 1 to 2 Compound Movements: 3 to 4 sets each. 5 to 10 reps per set.
  - 3 Exercise Circuit: Dumbbells, Bodyweight, or Machines.
  - 1 Trail Conditioning: 50 to 100 reps in 1 set.
  - 1 Core Finisher: Choose a core stability movement.

- **Day 2**
- **Elevation Day**
- **(Bodyweight, Athleticism Focus)**
  - Bodyweight Circuit for 20 to 40 minutes.

- **Day 3**
- **Approach Day**
- **(Steady-State Endurance)**
  - 30 to 60 minutes of steady-state cardio of choice.

- **Day 4**
- **Mountain-Strength 2**
- **(Upper Body Strength + Full Body Grind Circuit)**
  - 1 to 2 Compound Movements: 3 to 4 sets each. 5 to 10 reps per set.

- 3 Exercise Circuit: Dumbbells, Bodyweight, or Machines.
- 1 Trail Conditioning: 50 to 100 reps in 1 set.
- 1 Weighted Carry: Farmer's Carry, Sandbag Carry, and so on.

- **Day 5**
- **Backpack Day**
- **(Backpack Strength)**
  - Ruck with a loaded backpack for 30 to 90 minutes.
  - Progressively increase backpack weight and distance/time.
  - Aim for a daily mileage goal.

FOUR-DAY TRAINING SPLIT

- x 2 Mountain-Strength Days (with bodyweight "Elevation" circuits)
- x 1 Approach Day
- x 1 Backpack/Ruck/Hike Day

FOUR-DAY TEMPLATE

- **Day 1**
- **Mountain-Strength 1**
- **(Lower Body Strength + Upper Body Grind Circuit)**
  - 1 to 2 Compound Movements: 3 to 4 sets each. 5 to 10 reps per set.
  - 3 Exercise Circuit: Dumbbells, Bodyweight, or Machines.
  - 1 Trail Conditioning: 50 to 100 reps in 1 set.
  - 1 Core Finisher: Choose a core stability movement.

- **Day 2**
- **Approach Day**
- **(Steady-State Endurance)**
  - 30 to 60 minutes of steady-state cardio of choice.

- **Day 3**
- **Mountain-Strength 2**
- **(Upper Body Strength + Elevation Bodyweight Circuit)**

- 1 to 2 Compound Movements: 3 to 4 sets each. 5 to 10 reps per set.
- Elevation Circuit: Choose 3 to 6 athletic bodyweight exercises and complete as many rounds as possible in 15 to 20 minutes.
- 1 Trail Conditioning: 50 to 100 reps in 1 set.
- 1 Weighted Carry: Farmer's Carry, Sandbag Carry, and so on.

- **Day 4**
- **Backpack Day**
- **(Backpack Strength)**
  - Ruck with a loaded backpack for 30 to 90 minutes.
  - Progressively increase backpack weight and distance/time.
  - Aim for a daily mileage goal.

THREE-DAY TRAINING SPLIT

- x 2 Mountain-Strength Days (with bodyweight "Elevation" circuits)
- x 1 Approach Day (with added Ruck)

THREE-DAY TEMPLATE

- **Day 1**
- **Mountain-Strength 1**
- **(Lower Body Strength + Upper Body Grind Circuit)**
  - 1 to 2 Compound Movements: 3 to 4 sets each. 5 to 10 reps per set.
  - 3 Exercise Circuit: Dumbbells, Bodyweight, or Machines.
  - 1 Trail Conditioning: 50 to 100 reps in 1 set.
  - 1 Core Finisher: Choose a core stability movement.

- **Day 2**
- **Approach and Backpack Day**
- **(Steady-State Endurance + Ruck)**
  - 20 to 30 minutes of steady-state cardio of choice.
  - 20- to 30-minute ruck with a loaded backpack.
  - Progressively increase backpack weight and distance/time.
  - Aim for a daily mileage goal.

- **Day 3**
- **Mountain-Strength 2**
- **(Upper Body Strength + Elevation Bodyweight Circuit)**
  - 1 to 2 Compound Movements: 3 to 4 sets each. 5 to 10 reps per set.
  - Elevation Circuit: Choose 3 to 6 athletic bodyweight exercises and complete as many rounds as possible in 15 to 20 minutes.
  - 1 Trail Conditioning: 50 to 100 reps in 1 set.
  - 1 Weighted Carry: Farmer's Carry, Sandbag Carry, and so on.

TWO-DAY TRAINING SPLIT

- x 1 Mountain-Strength Day (with loaded backpack conditioning)
- x 1 Mountain-Strength Day (with "Elevation" + "Approach" conditioning)

TWO-DAY TEMPLATE

- **Day 1**
- **Mountain-Strength 1**
- **(Lower Body Strength + Upper Body Grind Circuit)**
  - 1 to 2 Compound Movements: 3 to 4 sets each. 5 to 10 reps per set.
  - 3 Exercise Circuit: Dumbbells, Bodyweight, or Machines.
  - 1 Trail Conditioning: 50 to 100 reps wearing loaded backpack.
  - 1 Core Finisher: Choose a core stability movement.

- **Day 2**
- **Mountain-Strength 2**
- **(Upper Body Strength + Elevation Bodyweight Circuit)**
  - 1 to 2 Compound Movements: 3 to 4 sets each. 5 to 10 reps per set.
  - Elevation Circuit: Choose 3 to 6 athletic bodyweight exercises and complete as many rounds as possible in 15 to 20 minutes.
  - Approach Steady State Conditioning: 15 to 20 minutes.
  - 1 Weighted Carry: Farmer's Carry, Sandbag Carry, and so on.

Chapter 7

The Summit

In hiking, the *summit* is the top of the mountain you've been working for the entire climb. It's where the effort, grit, and persistence all pay off. The views are breathtaking, but what makes the summit special isn't just the scenery—it's knowing you earned it. Every step, every struggle, every inch of trail, and every ounce of effort led you here. And you could have turned around at any point—but you didn't. Well done.

Becoming Unstoppable—on the Trail and in Your Life
Welcome to the final ascent of your *Hike Strong* experience. At the beginning of this book you signed in at the trailhead and committed to this journey to build strength and endurance for long hikes, steep climbs, and rugged terrain. Along the way, you learned that true strength isn't just physical. It's mental too. It's the ability to push forward when everything inside you is telling you to quit and go home. If you're reading this it means you've stayed the course and made it this far in the book, and I commend you for finishing what you started. This mindset will serve you well on the trail.

By now, you've realized this process has been about far more than just hiking and getting in better shape for hiking. It's been about building a stronger version of you inside and out that can confidently take on any challenge on a trail or in your life.

You've learned the fundamentals of training for mountain-strength and endurance so that no stone is left unturned in your trail fitness. You've developed a strategy to fuel your body for peak performance anywhere you go. You know exactly what to focus on to recover properly so you can show up stronger every day. But most importantly, you've built the mental toughness to keep going when things get hard. There are no participation trophies in the backcountry or the gym—every step, every rep, and every summit is earned. I know you're ready to earn those summits, and what a privilege it is to do so.

Your Strongest Self Is Just Ahead

So you've put in the work. You've built a strong, athletic body with a strong, resilient mind to go with it. But this is just the beginning for you. Your life's adventure story is still being written, and thankfully you're the one holding the pen. Again, what an awesome privilege it is.

So here's your final assignment before you close this book: Continue building mountain-strength, and set off on your next adventure.

The Final Ascent:

1. **Set a Hard Goal:** Pick a hike, a mountain, a trail, or an adventure that pushes you beyond what you think you're capable of. Something that makes you a little nervous committing to out loud. Then commit to it and believe in yourself.
2. **Train and Fuel with Intention:** Follow the principles and strategies you've learned in this book and execute with purpose and consistency. Strength, endurance, nutrition, recovery, and mindset are all critical pieces to the puzzle.
3. **Adopt a No-Quit Mentality:** Expect it to be hard. Expect obstacles to arise. Expect self-doubt to creep in. Then push through anyway. Remember to just focus on taking the next step . . . then another . . . then another. You'll learn that you're stronger than you ever knew.
4. **Look for the Lessons:** The trail will teach you something new every time you step onto it. Be open to learning those lessons and, most importantly, apply them to your life beyond the trail.

If there's one thing you take away from this book and this strength training journey, let it be this:

The mountains and the gym are the two greatest classrooms the world has to offer. They give you the tools to become your best self.

You now have a plan to execute within this book. You no longer have to spin your wheels in the gym or worry about whether your fitness will hold you back on the trail. Instead you are going to show up at every trailhead confident your legs and lungs will take you where you want to go because you are a mountain athlete now. And you deserve strong, fulfilling mountain adventures.

The Summit

James on a perfect winter day with fluffy snow.

I want you to write this next sentence down on a piece of paper and put it in your hiking pack and your gym bag as a reminder on the hard days:

A strong body builds a strong mind, and a strong mind builds a strong life.

You're not just training for hiking, and you're not just hiking for views, you're transforming into the strong, confident, adventurous person you're destined to become.

Now go. Train hard. Lift heavy. Hike strong. And live fully.

Strong mountain adventures await you.

Thanks for reading.

I'll see you on the trails!

Mountain-Strength Success Stories

"While I loved hiking and backpacking, I always struggled on my hikes. Years of long days sitting at a desk and eating poorly were not only holding me back in the outdoors but they were also killing my ability to excel in everyday life. At 60 years old, I had lost a substantial amount of muscle. Previous attempts (there were many) to get in shape were isolated to cardio-only programs, and while I lost some weight, I also lost even more muscle. I was in a downward spiral, running out of time, and needed to figure out a new approach.

Strength training completely changed the trajectory of my health and capability. The best part was the mindset shift though. I went from chasing pounds lost on the scale to chasing pounds added on the barbell. That change gave me small wins almost every day in my workouts, which kept me motivated and consistent. I've now been in James' Seek To Do More 1-on-1 program for a year, and the real superpower of strength training is how easy it becomes to stay consistent once you commit. It creates a true shift in mindset and discipline.

The improvements on the trail were dramatic. I like to backpack, and the difference was easy to measure. Yes I was able to hike more miles in a day, but more importantly I still felt strong at the end of the day. Still feeling like I had more in the tank at the end of the day was a big difference for me. Then other small wins added up too, like the ability to confidently hike on top of rocks instead of awkwardly stepping around them, a change I attribute to better strength, endurance, and athleticism. James' training accounts for all those things and the results speak for themself.

Beyond the trail, many of my everyday aches and pains disappeared too, and everyday life tasks like lugging 80 lbs of salt into the basement became easier. At 61, I'm now working on section-hiking the Appalachian Trail. Strength training is the secret sauce to 'not letting the old man in.'"

—**Dave Collins (Connecticut)**
Appalachian Trail Section Hiker

"When I first started hiking and backpacking, I was struggling to keep up with my goals. I wanted to explore further, move faster, and truly experience the beauty of the trail but my fitness was holding me back. I knew I needed something that would help me push through my perceived limitations.

I heard James on a podcast and that's when I found the Great Range Athlete Program. The combination of strength training and athletic movements was exactly what I needed. It replicated the demands of the trail, challenging my body in ways that made me stronger, faster, and more resilient. As I worked through the program, I found myself climbing faster, covering longer distances, and recovering quicker—allowing me to take on even more adventures.

The program transformed me into a more capable version of myself, unlocking new levels of strength and endurance I never thought possible. It's not just about reaching the summit, it's about completing the journey with strength, confidence, and a relentless drive to explore further.

After Great Range Athlete I continued working with James in his Seek To Do More program and my mindset and fitness level continues to soar to new heights. In six months I went from the couch and struggling on small local hikes, to losing over 25 lbs, confidently climbing High Peaks, completing ultra hikes, and I even ran my first half-marathon and competed in my first powerlifting meet. My mind is sharper than ever and the sky has become the limit for what I'm capable of. That's an amazing feeling."

—Annie Sumi (Maryland)

"I always thought I was a good hiker since I was born and raised in Colorado and used to the elevation. The truth is I was usually gassed halfway through most trails and thought that was just normal. What I didn't realize until I joined James' "Great Range Athlete" program was that while my general fitness level was ok, my strength wasn't where it needed to be to truly enjoy my hikes the way I wanted.

The first two weeks of the program were tough I will admit. I was sore, tired, and breaking old habits. But by week three, everything changed. I hiked a trail I'd done many times before and felt stronger, less exhausted, and more energized than ever. By the end of the program, I wasn't just finishing hikes but I was excelling on them, with energy to spare. This was a new revelation and experience altogether.

If you think you're a good hiker now, just wait until you see what strength training does for you. It completely changed the game for me."

—Cody "Codeman" Madsen
(Colorado)

"In December 2023 I walked in the room where I keep all of my hiking gear and decided to try on my hiking outfit. The one outfit that makes me come alive and fired up for what's to come on the trail. But this time that outfit was so tight I could barely get my shirt buttoned due to weight gain following my foot surgery. As a backpacker whose joy is found on the trail, I had to make a change. That was the day I made the decision to reach out to James and seek his help and guidance with losing weight and getting back in shape for hiking and life.

I needed a coach and I joined James' Seek To Do More program and little by little I began to notice changes in my body, strength, and most importantly, my mindset. I found that I CAN do more on a daily basis and having daily goals has been key to my success.

That summer (2024) I had the best summer of hiking because I was physically and mentally prepared. I found that hiking was the reward for all of the preparation, not the struggle that I was used to. Originally I sought to lose weight to go hiking, but I gained so much more strength and mental clarity than I ever thought possible.

The Seek To Do More Program has and will continue to sharpen my mind and body on a daily basis, on top of having amazing hikes. Thank You James!"

—Julie "Jester" Gayheart (North Carolina)
Two-Time Appalachian Trail Completer

"After being diagnosed with incurable cancer nearly nine years ago, my entire world shifted. Treatments undermined my body's ability to build and maintain muscle and bone, and every day became about putting one foot in front of the other just to lessen the risk of a much larger systemic decline.

I had always loved the Adirondacks, but even after years in Colorado, I knew I wasn't ready for the kind of rugged, steep, unpredictable trails of the Northeast. That's when I came across James Appleton and his Great Range Athlete program. I joined the 'Gothics' team in Fall 2024, and from that point, everything changed.

The GRA workouts are simple and accessible, but they're not easy and they're not supposed to be. James often reminds us 'climbing mountains is not easy either.' What surprised me most wasn't just the physical gains, but the way I reengaged with myself. I wasn't just maintaining anymore. I was progressing. I had doubts at first and had to modify things, but the team support and James' guidance made it all work.

When we finally hiked Gothics Peak in October it was wet, cold, snowy, windy, painful hips, and I even ripped pants, but I didn't doubt we'd make it. My team didn't doubt it. James didn't doubt it. I summited last, and they were all waiting and cheering.

Am I stronger now? Yes. Do I have more trail sense and ability? Absolutely. But more than anything, what I've carried forward from GRA is a calm, solid trust in myself on the trail, and in my life. Oh, and a new appreciation for good hiking pants too."

—Joe "JOHIO" Molloy (Ohio)

"Before joining James' Great Range Athlete program, I struggled with confidence on the trail especially when it came to hiking alone. I had anxiety around navigation, safety, and overall physical preparedness. But through the strength training program and weekly coaching calls, I got physically stronger and I became a more confident, capable, and informed hiker as well.

I've always considered myself a well-rounded athlete, but James' program humbled me in the best way. I expected it to feel easy after years of CrossFit, but the muscle soreness and real GAINS reminded me that you have to keep challenging yourself if you want to keep growing.

Now, I feel stronger head to toe, more confident stepping into the woods, and proud of how far I've come. Lifting weights gave me a different kind of endorphin high than running marathons and now as an official GRA grad, I'll never let the weights collect dust again."

—Mallory Michaels (New York)
Four-Time Marathon Finisher

"When it comes to training regimens in the current day, the temptation and focus of many coaches and trainees is to put too much focus on a singular aspect of training, instead of having a well-rounded regimen. With cardiovascular endurance being the rule of the day for the last couple decades, it was refreshing to go through James' Great Range Athlete program because it struck a near-perfect balance of strength and endurance woven into each week of training.

Joining James' Great Range Athlete 'Colden Team' was perfect timing. I was growing tired of my own workout routines that I'd been implementing for years following my service as a medic in the U.S. Army. Throughout the GRA program, and in the days following, I continue to feel a renewed strength and endurance in my climbing, skiing, and hiking pursuits.

GRA was the perfect kickstart to move me in a new focused direction for my current and future work in guiding, backcountry emergency medicine, and search and rescue."

—Mark Anderson (California)
Aspirant AMGA Guide, NYS Licensed Guide, EMT,
10th MTN Army Veteran

"As a middle-aged mother who works at a desk all day, I was getting frustrated with my hiking ability. No matter how much cardio I was doing I would plateau without any more strength. Invariably, I was disappointed each summer as my planned hikes would end up harder than I expected. On the trail my heart would be pounding and my legs would be sluggish. This made no sense to me. Last year was kind of the final straw after getting walloped going uphill in the Catskills on a hike that took me days to recover from. Then I heard about James and his Great Range Athlete training program. His story resonated with me, and I thought this may be my solution.

For sure I was intimidated. The GRA program is tough, but I did it. I made it through and I got stronger than I could have imagined even a few months ago. My legs feel great! My balance is better! I've already done hikes that I thought were too hard for me before. After going through the Great Range Athlete program, I am prepared to be a better hiker and uphill athlete. I've made so much progress, and now I know how to train my body for strong hiking. There will never be another plateau for my fitness, and I feel confident that I can choose to go on any hike I want. The overall health benefits are amazing for all parts of my life. A great bonus is that I have a community of like-minded outdoor athletes as friends through the GRA program. James really created an amazing program! I am forever grateful that I got involved with Great Range Athlete."

—Ann Shincovich (Pennsylvania)

"For years, I have been struggling my way up the High Peaks of the Adirondacks on my quest to become a 46er. With the shorter, easier High Peaks crossed off my list and the remaining hikes being much more difficult, my goal was beginning to seem unattainable. So I decided to join one of James' team programs and try his strength-based fitness program to improve my ability in the backcountry. I quickly noticed substantial improvements on the trail where years of endless cardio had failed. Now, those brutal slogs lasting into the night with days of painful recovery to follow turned into enjoyable and fulfilling adventures with plenty of daylight to spare. I'm now reminded of why I fell in love with hiking in the first place. Thanks to this newfound strength and confidence on trail I expect to become an Adirondack 46er in the near future and look forward to the next challenge."

—Scott Henninger (Pennsylvania)

"Knee pain has always been my biggest issue with hiking. I'd experience it after any strenuous activity or long hike. But once I joined the GRA program, everything changed. The workouts, advice, and motivation from other athletes helped me finally start building real mountain fitness.

At first squats gave me pain. But after learning how to correctly modify the movement for my needs it made all the difference. It gave me the chance to strengthen the area without overdoing it. Now, I'm doing full squats with a loaded backpack or kettlebell and I'm completely pain-free. That's a massive improvement for me.

At the end of the program, I did a winter hike in the Adirondack High Peaks on Mt. Colvin. As you know, a winter pack is a lot heavier than a summer one with all the extra gear, but I felt strong the entire day. Also noteworthy is that I hiked another mountain the day before too with one of my GRA teammates. Two hikes, back-to-back, and still no knee pain.

On top of the physical gains, the program introduced me to an incredible group of hikers who care about fitness and pushing themselves. I've built real strength and I'm honestly the strongest I've ever been. I've also made great friendships with my teammates along the way."

—**Jon L. (Ohio)**

"I was trying to get in shape to thru hike the Appalachian Trail and knew I needed a fitness routine. I live in North Dakota and realized how difficult it would be to get a personal trainer who has specific hiking knowledge and expertise here in my hometown. I found James on a podcast where he was talking about how strength training will improve your ability to go hiking. He mentioned his six week training program and I decided to sign up. I'm so glad I did! James' coaching pushed us to go above and beyond what we thought we could do and now I feel much stronger and more confident to tackle the 2,200 miles of the A.T. next month. Thank you, James!"

—**Beth Stenehjem (North Dakota)**
Appalachian Trail Thru Hiker

"For a long time I struggled with hiking confidently—what I mean by that is, at some point during a backcountry hike, I would feel doubt or fear creeping in. Doubt that I would be able to complete the hike, and fear of being deep in the wilderness.

I've tried different strength programs before, but for one reason or another I would fall off, switch to something else, or get bored with the monotony. James' Great Range Athlete program caught me by surprise, in the best way possible. The GRA program was the exact opposite of anything I've done in the past—it was challenging on both a physical and mental level, and it kept me engaged throughout the six weeks because of the variety and creativity of the workouts, coupled with the team-like mentality that kept everyone accountable.

My results were as much confidence-based as they were strength-based. I found that my strength improved on a functional level—I could carry more weight on my back, my knees felt stronger, and my core felt more stable. All of these factors directly impacted my confidence on the trail and gave me an improved hiking foundation that I can continue to build on. I can't say enough about this program!"

—**Nicole Komin (New York)**

"I realized I needed a specific training program to become a stronger hiker, but trainers just told me to hike more. Knowing that wasn't working, I researched and created my own program, which helped but wasn't to the level I wanted to achieve. Then, I started working with James 1-on-1, who designed a strength training program tailored to my needs. Because of his coaching and Seek To Do More I now feel stronger, hike longer distances, navigate tough terrain better, and recover faster after hikes. Thanks to his training that mimics trail conditions I'm now a stronger hiker which has allowed me to set higher goals and I have fun doing them."

—**Amanda Fischer (Wisconsin)**
Ice Age Trail Finisher and Steward

"I'm a 66 year old hiker and I have some hiking experience, but I lacked confidence on the trail. That's why I joined the Great Range Athlete program and it kicked my butt right from day one. I'm proud to say though I did every workout and couldn't believe the progress I made week after week. I gained a ton of knowledge about hiking, training, and nutrition. I also gained a bunch of new hiking friends who've become like a little family. I trusted the process and got stronger and wiser. I got that confidence and I reclaimed the athlete I once was. I'm stronger and ready to hike anytime. I'm a better person now all around thanks to James and the Great Range Athletes."

—**Stephen LaFave (New York)**
Marathon Finisher

The Descent

In hiking, the *descent* is the journey back down the mountain. Your legs are tired, your feet are muddier, and your pack is lighter, but your heart is full. You walk down the mountain with a newfound confidence. Sure, there may still be miles to hike back to the trailhead, but it's different now. You've done the hard thing. You stood on the summit. You saw what you're capable of.

No matter how many times you hike a mountain you never come down the same person who went up. You come down stronger. Clearer. A little more transformed. And that, my friends, is the beauty of the backcountry. Because somewhere between the sweat, the trees, the heavy breathing, and the views, you walk out better than you walked in.

There's magic in the mountains. Now go experience it!

About the Author

James doing what he does best: guiding others to become their strongest selves in the mountains and in their lives.

James Appleton, S&C, is a New York State licensed hiking and camping guide (#8790) and an International Sports Sciences Association (ISSA) certified strength and conditioning coach. He holds state powerlifting records, has won several competitions in powerlifting and strongman, and has run many half-marathons.

On the trail, James has hiked multiple rounds of the Adirondack 46 High Peaks, backpacked the Northville-Placid Trail, and completed the mighty Great Range Traverse in the Adirondacks. He's the founder of the Lake Placid 9'er, a low peak hiking challenge that introduces people to hiking in the ADK.

To date James has helped over three thousand hikers have successful mountain adventures. He's personally coached hundreds of people around the United States and Canada helping them get strong, fit, and prepared

About the Author

for hiking and backpacking. His passion lies in guiding others to transform their lives, just like he did, through strength training and the great outdoors.

Beyond the trail and gym . . .

James is a best-selling author who has two other published books, *The Adirondack 46 in 18 Hikes: The Complete Guide to Hiking the High Peaks* and *Adirondack Campfire Stories: Tales and Folklore from Inside the Blue Line*. As a natural-born storyteller, James hosts *The 46 of 46 Podcast*, the premiere podcast that brings the mountains, lakes, rivers, and stories of the Adirondack Park to life.

Before founding the 46 Outdoors Company and Seek To Do More, he worked in Hollywood for seventeen years as a production sound mixer and boom operator with over one hundred feature film and television credits including Academy Award– and Emmy-winning productions.

He lives a simple life in the heart of the Adirondack Mountains in the Olympic town of Lake Placid, New York, with his wife and three daughters.

Work With James

If *Hike Strong* lit a fire in you, then this is just the beginning.

Whether you're preparing for your first summit, chasing your next big adventure, or striving to become the strongest version of yourself, you don't have to do it alone.

Through my **SEEK TO DO MORE 1-on-1 coaching program**, I work closely with adventurous and driven people who are ready to transform to become unstoppable on the trail and in their life. With Seek To Do More you'll not only get customized training for the outdoors built to fit into your schedule and lifestyle but we'll also dive deep into nutrition, mindset, daily habits, and everything in between. This is for those who are ready to go all in on themselves to become their best and want high-level support, accountability, and mentorship every step of the way.

Apply to Work with James one on one at
www.SeekToDoMore.com.

Do you prefer the energy and camaraderie of a team? Then join one of my **GREAT RANGE ATHLETE group programs**—built for mountain athletes just like you. These online groups help hikers level up their fitness for the backcountry through strength and conditioning programs tailored for hikers, backpackers, and outdoor adventurers. You'll get the structure and coaching you need, the outdoors education and community you've been craving, and the strength gains to carry you further than ever before. These teams are for all experience and fitness levels. Whether you're starting from the couch or you're a seasoned hiker, there's always a next level waiting for you. Let's go find it together.

Join the Team at
www.GreatRangeAthlete.com.

HIKE STRONG

Connect With James:

www.46outdoors.com

james@46outdoors.com

@jamesappleton46

@46Outdoors

The 46 of 46 Podcast

www.46outdoors.com

Hike Strong Exercise Library

There are hundreds of impactful exercises to choose from to get your body strong and fit for the trail. This library has some of my favorites and includes all of the exercises from the *Hike Strong* training programs. The movements are listed in alphabetical order.

"Backcountry" Burpees

- Perform a standard burpee, but after standing, do a step-up onto a box or bench. Step down and repeat, alternating legs each rep.

Barbell Overhead Press

- Hold a barbell at shoulder height with palms facing forward. Press the bar overhead until arms are fully extended, then lower the bar back down under control. Can be seated on a bench or standing in a squat rack.

Barbell Squat

- Stand with feet shoulder-width apart and a barbell resting on your upper back. Take in and hold a breath of air, brace your core, keep a neutral spine, and squat down until your thighs are parallel with the floor. Keep your chest up and knees in line with toes. Push through your heels to return to standing.

Bent-over Row

- Hold a barbell or dumbbells with a slight bend in your knees. Hinge at your hips while keeping your back flat. Pull the weight toward your ribcage by driving your elbows back. Lower under control. Imagine your elbows pulling the weight back and then stop once your elbows hit 90 degrees.

Bench Press (Barbell or Dumbbell)

- Lie on a bench with a barbell or dumbbells over your chest. Lower the weight under control, keeping elbows at a 45-degree angle. Press back up to the starting position.

Biceps Curls (Dumbbell)

- Hold a dumbbell in each hand with palms facing forward. Curl the weights toward your shoulders while keeping elbows close to your torso. Lower back down slowly.

Bodyweight Squats

- Stand with feet shoulder-width apart. Lower your hips down and back as if sitting in a chair, keeping your chest up. Push through your heels to return to standing.

Burpees

- Start standing, then squat down and place your hands on the ground. Jump or step your feet back into a push-up position. Perform a push-up (optional), then jump or step your feet back to your hands and explode into a jump at the top.

Calf Raises (Bodyweight or Dumbbell)

- Stand with feet hip-width apart. Press through the balls of your feet to lift your heels as high as possible, squeeze your calves at the top, then lower back down slowly.

Chest Press (Dumbbell)

- Lie on a bench with a dumbbell in each hand. Lower the weights until your elbows are at a 90-degree angle, then press them back up.

Chest-Supported Row (Dumbbell or Machine)

- Lie chest down on an incline bench while holding dumbbells. Pull the weights toward your rib cage until your elbow forms 90 degrees, squeezing your shoulder blades together. Lower the dumbbells under control.

Hike Strong Exercise Library

Farmer Carry (Dumbbell)

- Hold a heavy dumbbell in each hand and walk a set distance while keeping your core braced and shoulders back. While walking, breathe in through your nose and out through your mouth to keep your core tight. Imagine breathing out through a straw.

Flutter Kicks

- Lie on your back with legs fully extended. Lift your feet slightly off the ground and alternate small kicks in a scissor-like motion while engaging your core. Keep your hands under your glutes for balance.

Goblet Squat (Dumbbell or Kettlebell)

- Hold a dumbbell at chest height with both hands. Lower into a squat while keeping the weight close to your chest and torso upright. Push through your heels to return to standing.

Hack Squat Machine

- Position yourself in the hack squat machine with feet shoulder-width apart. Lower into a squat while keeping your back against the pad. Push through your heels to return to the starting position.

High Knees

- Stand tall and run in place, bringing your knees up to waist height with each step. Tap each knee as you raise it and maintain a quick pace.

Incline Bench Press (Dumbbell or Barbell)

- Lie on an incline bench with a dumbbell in each hand. Lower the weights under control, then press them back up while keeping your chest engaged.

"Jester" Lunge and Press

- Hold a loaded backpack or weight in front of your chest. Step into a lunge, and at the bottom of the movement, press the weight overhead. Lower it back down before standing up. Alternate legs each rep.

"Jester" Press

- Hold a loaded backpack or weight at chest height. Press it overhead until arms are fully extended, then lower it back to the starting position. Maintain a strong core and stable stance.

"Jester" Squat

- Hold a loaded backpack or weight against your chest. Lower into a squat, keeping your torso upright. Push through your heels to return to standing while maintaining control of the weight.

Jump Lunges

- Start in a lunge position with one foot forward and the other behind. Explode upward, switching legs mid-air, and land softly in a lunge with the opposite foot forward. Repeat.

Jump Squats

- Stand with feet shoulder-width apart. Lower into a squat, then explode up, jumping as high as possible. Land softly and go straight into the next rep. Find a rhythm and maintain it for the set.

Jumping Jacks

- Start standing with feet together and arms at your sides. Jump your feet out while bringing your arms overhead. Return to the starting position and repeat. Jumping jacks are the ultimate warm-up before your workout to get your entire body moving.

Lat Pull-Downs (Cable or Machine)

- Sit at a lat pull-down machine and grip the bar slightly wider than shoulder width. Pull the bar down to your chest while keeping your back straight, then slowly return it. A helpful cue to ensure your lats are doing the work includes thinking about your elbows pulling the weight down, not your arms.

Leg Press Machine

- Sit in the leg press machine and place your feet shoulder-width apart on the platform. Press the weight up until your legs are almost straight, then slowly lower back down without locking out your knees.

Lunges (Dumbbell)

- Hold a dumbbell in each hand and step forward into a lunge, lowering your back knee toward the ground. Push through your front foot to return to standing. There are many variations (front, side, back, walking, etc.) and they're all useful. Some variations may feel better than others.

Mountain Climbers

- Start in a push-up position with your hands under your shoulders. Drive one knee toward your chest, then quickly switch legs in a running motion. Keep your core engaged and back straight.

Overhead Press (Dumbbell)

- Hold a dumbbell in each hand at shoulder height. Press the weights overhead until arms are fully extended, then lower them back down. Can be seated on a bench of standing.

Plank (Forearm or High Position)

- Get into a forearm plank position with elbows under shoulders and feet hip-width apart. Engage your core and glutes while keeping your back straight. Hold for the prescribed time without letting your hips sag. A cue to engage your core properly includes imagining bringing your belt buckle to your chest.

Pull-Ups (Assisted or Bodyweight)

- Grab a pull-up bar with an overhand, underhand, or neutral grip. Pull yourself up until your chin clears the bar, then lower back down slowly. Use a resistance band or machine if needed.

Push-Ups

- Begin in a high plank position with hands slightly wider than shoulder width. Lower your chest toward the floor while keeping your elbows at a 45-degree angle. Press back up to the starting position. Modify by dropping to your knees or perform against a raised bench if needed.

Rear Foot Elevated Split Squat (Dumbbell)

- Hold a dumbbell in each hand and place one foot behind you on a bench. Lower into a split squat by bending the front knee. Push through your front foot to return to standing.

Romanian Deadlift (Dumbbell)

- Hold a dumbbell in each hand in front of your thighs. Hinge back at your hips, lowering the weights down your legs while keeping your back straight. Stand up by driving your hips forward and squeezing your glutes and hamstrings.

Ruck (Loaded Backpack Carry)

- Wear a weighted backpack and walk for a designated time or distance. Maintain good posture and a steady pace.

Shrugs (Dumbbell)

- Hold a dumbbell in each hand at your sides. Lift your shoulders toward your ears, squeeze for a few seconds, then lower them under control.

Side Lunges

- Stand with feet wider than hip-width apart. Shift your weight to one leg, lowering into a side lunge while keeping the other leg straight. Push back to the center and repeat on the other side.

Single-Arm Row (Dumbbell)

- Place one hand on a bench for support and hold a dumbbell in the opposite hand. Pull the weight toward your torso by driving your elbow back, keeping your back straight. Lower under control and switch sides.

Skater Jumps

- Start in a slight squat. Jump laterally to one side, landing softly on one foot while bringing the other foot behind you. Immediately jump to the other side and repeat.

Step-Ups (Bodyweight or Weighted)

- Step onto a box or bench with one leg, driving through the heel to lift yourself up. Step down with control and repeat on the other leg. A good height to aim for is fifteen to twenty inches.

Trap Bar Deadlift

- Stand inside a trap bar, also called a hex bar, and grip the handles. Drive through your heels to lift the weight while keeping your chest up and back straight. Lower the bar under control. Good cues include imagining squeezing tennis balls under your armpits to activate your lats, and imagining pushing the floor away from you, rather than standing up. This "pushing the floor away" cue will help activate the glutes, hamstrings, and quads.

Wall Sit

- Lean against a wall with your feet shoulder width apart and your knees at 90 degrees so your thighs are parallel to the floor. Keep your back flat against the wall and hold for the designated time.

Acknowledgments

THANK YOU to . . .

My wife, Kinnon, and my daughters, June, Penny, and Rosemary, for being on this journey of life with me. You are my world and leading you has been my greatest adventure.

All of my **Seek To Do More** and **Great Range Athlete** clients around the United States and Canada for following my lead and proving the Mountain-Strength Method works every time you hit the trail. Watching you all grow physically and mentally stronger—and have more fulfilling hiking adventures on top of that—is a privilege I do not take for granted. I am grateful for all of you. Keep showing up for yourselves every day.

The Adirondack Park and Shedside Barbell for transforming me into the man I am today.

—Dr. Tyler Cook for being my early morning soundboard, my accountability partner every writing session, and for writing your next book alongside me. I'm blessed to have your support, wisdom, encouragement, and brotherhood. It's done. Punching out.

—J. E. Appleton for your contributions during the editing process of another one of my books.

—My parents and siblings for their endless support.

—Jonathan Zaharek Photography for the photos throughout this book.

—Josh Bliss for being both my training and hiking partner. #RepsForBull

The Piano Guys Radio Pandora station for setting the musical vibe every writing session here at Shedquarters.

ACKNOWLEDGMENTS

And most importantly . . .

Thank YOU for reading this book. May all of your adventures be stronger than ever. Don't be afraid to pass this book along to someone else who can benefit from it too. Because everyone deserves to have strong mountain adventures.

www.ingramcontent.com/pod-product-compliance
Ingram Content Group UK Ltd.
Pitfield, Milton Keynes, MK11 3LW, UK
UKHW041922210426
5322IPUK00001B/2